I Can Do
Rhythmic Gymnastics:
Floor, Rope and Ball

USA Gymnastics
in cooperation with the
Federacion Espanola de Gimnasia

A Division of Howard W. Sams & Company

Published by Masters Press
A Division of Howard W. Sams & Company
2647 Waterfront Pkwy E. Drive
Indianapolis, IN 46214

Printed in the United States of America.

96 97 98 99 00 01   10 9 8 7 6 5 4 3 2 1

Library of Congress Cataloging-in-Publication Data

Gimnasia ritmica.   English.
    I can do rhythmic gymnastics: floor, rope and ball / USA Gymnastics in cooperation with the Federacion Espanola de Gimnasia.
        p.   cm.
    ISBN 1-57028-051-7 (trade paper)
    1. Rhythmic gymnastics. I. U.S.A. Gymnastics. II. Federacion Espanola de Gimnasia.   III. Title.
GV463.G56   1997   97-35586
796.44--dc21   CIP

Table of Contents

Acknowledgments

USA Gymnastics would like to acknowledge several people for all their hard work in bringing *I Can Do Rhythmic Gymnastics: Floor, Rope and Ball* into its final form. Without their talents and dedication, this book would not be in existence.

Authors of the original Spanish edition: Susana and Isabel Mendizabal

Translation of the original text into English: Graciella Yanas

Editor, USA Gymnastics edition: Nora Campbell

Assitant Editor, USA Gymnastics edition: Paula Lord

Illustrators: Mary Burkhart, Jan Williamson and Amy Kirchner

Models for game and skill illustration photos from Rhythmflex Gymnastics and the Oregon Gymnastics Academy

Game and skill illustration photos taken by Keiko Guest

Credits:

Cover design: Debra Wilson

Cover photos: © Dave Black Photography

I Can Do
Rhythmic Gymnastics:
Floor, Rope and Ball

Chapter One
Rhythmic Floor

Discussions about rhythmic gymnastics primarily focus attention on the equipment: rope, hoop, ball, clubs and ribbon; without taking into account the required base for the gymnast's preparation: rhythmic floor.

What is rhythmic floor? Using an analogy, it is like the trunk and branches of a tree that are in continuous growth. Following its development, the tree first takes root, getting ready to hold and feed the trunk. This is analogous to the preparatory exercises which will be mentioned briefly in Chapter 1.

Little by little the trunk emerges, growing and constantly getting stronger. The trunk represents the different groups of floor exercise elements which form the basic technique. With a minimum of training, using the preparatory exercises, the basic technique can be introduced. The basic technique is formed by elements that may seem simple but require the use of a determined technique in order to be performed. That technique is generally adapted to each group of elements and, at the same time, to each element in particular. An increase in difficulty and possible combinations between elements can be achieved by improving this technique. Training in this way achieves technical preparation for each element, coordination with other movements, and the possibility of combining the learned moves with the handling of equipment.

1

In the trunk of the tree, little by little the branches begin to show up. These are the different apparatus that make up rhythmic gymnastics, which will be progressively introduced according to the apparatus' difficulty.

The preparatory exercises, mentioned before, are the positions and movements of the arms and legs as learned through a combination of techniques from classical dance and specific physical training—a very important issue that will not be treated here.

Now, assuming a base of physical training and ballet has been established, the basic technique is the next area of study.

BASIC TECHNIQUE

√ Traveling steps √ Swinging and circular motions

√ Torso motions and waves √ Balances

√ Turns √ Jumps

√ Pre-acrobatics

Various *traveling steps* and short runs are used to move along the carpet in all directions, in either straight or curved lines. Also, they unify the most difficult elements and give moments of amplitude, rhythm and motion to the composition.

Swinging and circular motions with the arms, in conjunction with the movement and position of the hands, are very important because correct posture and good expression can help to determine the level of a gymnast.

Movement of the torso must be followed by movement of the arms and hands, giving continuity to the flexion of the torso. These are elements which show the main characteristics of flexibility and elasticity—waves. Waves are unique and specific elements of rhythmic gymnastics, wide and relaxed movements which demonstrate, in contrast with fast movements, great control of the whole body. Waves are frequently forgotten in training.

Balances are elements whose development is based on preparatory elements, primarily from classical dance. It is very important to obtain, little by little, balance of the body in all possible positions to be able to perform turns.

Turns may be defined as balance in motion, spinning around a vertical axis, combining both into a single element. This is often the hardest group of elements for a gymnast.

Jumps are an entity of a composition which cannot be replaced. Due to the wide variety of jumps that exist, the amount of usable space on the carpet increases, not only in terms of horizontal travel but also vertical travel. This variety provides color, motion, speed and definition to the composition.

Pre-acrobatics, despite their difficulty, are not included in the rhythmic gymnastics code as a group of elements. Nevertheless, they will be included as another group in the basic technique, and will be given the same consideration in methods of training and development.

When the groups of elements are combined and adapted to music, they make a perfect and harmonious rhythmic gymnastics presentation.

POSITIONS AND BASIC MOVES

Positions of the arms

We will differentiate:

√ Positions in classical dance

√ Positions in rhythmic gymnastics

√ Positions of the hands

POSITIONS IN CLASSICAL DANCE

The five positions of the arms in classical dance, along with positions of the legs and torso, help the gymnast to keep the correct posture. These positions are not used in the composition of an exercise.

Start position: Arms slightly rounded alongside the body.

First position: Form a circle with arms ahead of the body and below horizontal (low oblique).

Second position: Raise arms laterally, forming a line from one hand to the other across shoulders.

Third position: One arm slightly rounded overhead, other arm at the side aligned with shoulder.

Fourth position: Both arms rounded, one overhead, other arm ahead of the body and aligned with shoulder.

Fifth position: Both arms rounded and slightly forward overhead.

Practice shifting from one position to the next as follows:

From 1st to 2nd, raise and open both arms

From 2nd to 3rd, raise right arm

From 3rd to 4th, move left arm forward

From 4th to 5th, raise left arm

If the exercise is performed with the right leg forward, the positions of the arms are as previously mentioned. If the gymnast is working with the left leg forward, the left arm is raised to shift from 2nd to 3rd, and the right arm is moved forward and raised to shift from 3rd to 4th and from 4th to 5th.

POSITIONS OF THE ARMS IN RHYTHMIC GYMNASTICS

Both arms down
and stretched

Both arms rounded

One arm rounded and
the other stretched

Both arms up
and stretched

Both arms rounded

One arm rounded and
the other stretched

Both arms forward and
stretched

Both arms rounded

One arm rounded and
the other stretched

Arms to the sides and
stretched

Both arms rounded

One arm rounded and
the other stretched

Shifting from one position to another can be done with both arms simultaneously or by alternating arms. For a higher difficulty, shift the arms asymmetrically.

Hand Positions

It is necessary to know the positions of the hands, because an incorrect position will take value and harmony away from the movement.

The hands must be neither tense nor stiff (except when a specific position, determined by the character of the music, is to be performed).

A totally relaxed position of the hands, however, causes the movement to lose its continuity.

The hands must have enough tension to hold a correct position, yet remain sufficiently relaxed to have expression and to extend the movement of the arms. The ideal position is with the thumb close to the middle finger and the rest of the fingers slightly separated.

Arm Movements

The capacity of a gymnast to move her arms gracefully is one of the best ways to show the elegance of her own style.

Movement of the arms must always be in coordination with the rest of the body, and should be smooth and aesthetic. Arm movements must always be accompanied by the hands. Lack of coordination between arms and hands will affect the harmony of the movement.

Using the five arm positions in classical dance previously mentioned, gymnasts can learn smooth and coordinated movements.

There are three joints involved with arm movements: shoulder, elbow and wrist.

Before starting with the different, more complex and, therefore, more difficult to coordinate movements of the arms, it is recommended to work with each of these joints separately.

Shoulder Movements

Perform the movements starting as follows: seated on heels, knees together, and arms relaxed.

a) Raise both shoulders simultaneously, hold the contraction a few seconds, then relax. Repeat several times.

b) Elevate one shoulder while forcibly pushing the other shoulder downward toward the floor and alternate.

c) Circle both shoulders forward and backward.

d) Draw circles with shoulders, one at a time, alternately. Change the direction of the rotation.

Elbow Movements

Begin kneeling, right arm on floor, left arm relaxed.

a) Draw circles with the right elbow while the right hand is on the floor. Repeat with the left elbow.

b) Circle both elbows simultaneously and alternately.

In a standing position, keeping the arms stretched to the sides, draw circles from the elbow joint with forearm and perform:

c) Circles in frontal plane with one or two arms; simultaneously or alternately (both directions).

d) Circles in sagittal plane with one or two arms; simultaneously or alternately (both directions).

Wrist Movements

Stand with arms extended to the sides.

a) Move both hands upward and downward, simultaneously and alternately.

b) Circle both hands forward and backward, simultaneously and alternately.

c) Close and open both hands very quickly, simultaneously and alternately.

Positions of the Feet

Correct positions of the feet provide confidence in all movements. The classical positions of the feet accompany the arm positions previously mentioned. In rhythmic gymnastics the positions of the feet are slightly different. For instance, the 5th and 1st positions are not fully turned out. All of these positions are the basis of preparatory exercises.

It is suggested that the gymnast practice the exercises using a ballet barre, stall bars, or the back of a chair for support. Place one hand on the barre at about waist high. Once the exercise is mastered, it can be performed without support.

POSITIONS OF FEET IN CLASSICAL DANCE

The five positions of ballet.

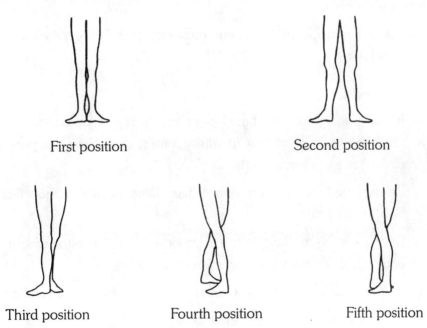

First position   Second position

Third position   Fourth position   Fifth position

While holding these positions it is important to:

√ Keep both arms relaxed

√ Keep hips straight and "open" (thigh muscles rotated outward)

√ Keep buttocks muscles contracted

√ Elevate torso

√ Push shoulders downward and lift chin

It is also important to have the weight equally distributed on the feet.

Leg Movements

PLIÉS (KNEE BENDING)

The movement of bending the knees is called plié. There are two types. Demi-plié is performed without lifting the heels, bending the knees only half-way. Grande plié is performed lifting the heels in 1st, 3rd, 4th and 5th, and holding them on the ground in 2nd position. The knees bend as far as possible while keeping a good body position.

Pliés are necessary for the take-off and landing technique of any jump. They allow the body's weight to be held correctly.

Exercises begin facing the barre, and once mastered, holding the barre at the side with one hand.

RELEVÉ (EXTENSIONS)

Relevé is the extension of the legs up to a high position on the ball of the foot. Relevé is important for the gymnast to achieve for performing pirouettes and turns correctly.

Relevé is performed on one or both feet, lifting the heels without flexing or bending the knees.

During a relevé on both legs it is important to balance the weight of the body evenly on both legs, never on only one leg.

As exercises, begin facing a barre. Grasp the barre with both hands and perform:

√ Four relevés in the five different positions

√ Combine a demi-plié (without lifting the heels) with a relevé

√ Repeat each position eight times

POSITIONS OF THE LEGS IN RHYTHMIC GYMNASTICS

Lunge: Flex one leg forward without lifting the heel. The other leg is extended backward to a pointed position. Keep the torso straight with weight on flexed leg. Perform the exercise with both legs.

Possible variations:

Forward   Sideward   Backward

a) Place the weight on one leg with the other leg stretched, flexed or bent.

Possible variations:

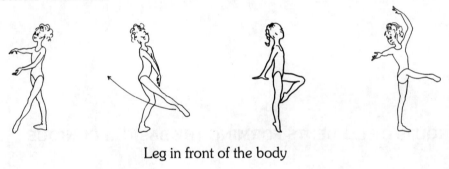

Leg in front of the body

To the side of the body

Behind the body

b) Kick the right leg upward and extended, flexed and bent in the different planes.

GROUPS OF ELEMENTS FORMING THE BASIC TECHNIQUE

Traveling Steps

This group is important because it works as a link between the rest of the groups, jumps, turns, balances, etc., and is the method of traveling along the carpet during the exercise. Traveling steps can be combined with any movement of the arms to provide beauty to the movement. There must be a great variety in the traveling steps, which can be performed in straight lines, curved, forward, sideways or backwards.

RHYTHMIC STEPS

a) <u>March-in steps.</u> With toes pointed and legs slightly rotated outward, walk swinging the arms from the shoulders (opposite arm to the leg in front). Shift the direction of the steps (forward, oblique, backward). The body is straight, legs tight, stomach pulled in, torso and chin lifted.

√ March-in with heel support   √ March-in without heel support, on toes

b) Smooth step. March-in step, sliding both legs smoothly, the toe touches the floor first and then the heel.

c) Piqué steps. Move the leg forward tapping the floor with the toe (with the leg flexed) and stretch to perform the step.

d) High step. Perform a march-in step on toes, kicking each leg to at least 45°.

e) Cross step [Grapevine].

Forward. Step with the right foot forward, step with the left foot crossed behind the right, and step forward again with the right. Start with the left foot.

Sideward. Step to the side with the right foot, step with the left foot to the rear, to the side with the right, and then to the front with the left.

f) Rolled step (with spring). March-in step, pushing with the foot to spring the leg from the floor. Lift the knee and change legs for each step.

g) Circle step. Slide the right foot from the rear to the front, drawing an imaginary semi-circle to the right. Shift weight from left to right foot, and then circle the left.

h) Lunge step. Make a large step forward, bending the front knee. Leg in the rear is extended. Do the same with the other leg (the arm opposite the leg in front is forward).

i) Chasse. Step with the right foot, join the left leg to the right, then step again with right. Reverse the step to the left by joining right leg to the left and then stepping again with the left.

j) Waltz step.

Forward: Step in demi-plié on the right leg. Take two steps forward, left then right, on the toes. The waltz step is to be performed in three counts.

Backward: Same as forward but step to the rear.

Sideward: Side step to the right in demi-plié. Cross left leg once to step behind, then step right in front on toes. Alternate right side step, left side step.

These steps can be done with or without travel. It is also possible to perform the waltz step with a small spring.

To increase the difficulty, a turn can be introduced in the waltz step.

k) Waltz step with turn. Step left in demi-plié. Complete a half turn to the left using the two intermediate steps. Step right in demi-plié stretching the left leg backward and complete the second half of the turn to the left with the two steps on toes.

Runs

All the varieties of steps previously mentioned can be done with runs.

a) Smooth run. Run with legs extended, toes pointed.

b) Piqué run. Similar to the piqué step, lift the knees to waist height before stepping forward.

c) Long run. The steps are long and close to the floor, kept in suspension due to the amplitude of the run step.

d) High run. These steps use the energy to kick the extended legs forward, with a small forward travel (scissors or hitch kick).

e) Cross run [Grapevine run]. With one leg step to the side as the other leg crosses once to the front and once to the rear.

f) Waltz rhythm run. Perform the waltz step with a short jump and two little runs (jump-step-step).

g) Chassé. Step forward on one leg to spring joining the other leg while in the air, landing on the leg in the rear.

  √ Chassé backward.

  √ Chassé side (right and left).

  √ Alternating chassés. Perform a series of chassés alternating legs, right and left.

h) Schottische step. Do three running steps. Lift one knee to perform a hop on the support leg. Begin the run with the raised-knee leg.

COMMON MISTAKES DURING THE EXECUTION OF TRAVELS AND METHODS OF CORRECTION

a) Knees and toes facing inward.

b) Lack of movement and rhythm during the travels.

Methods of correction for knees and toes facing inward

Both knees and toes must be open (turned out slightly) with the heels facing inward.

Exercises: On a straight line, perform all the steps, placing the toes outside the line and heels on the line.

Examples:

√ Four march-in steps with heel support, four march-in steps on toes

√ Four march-in steps on toes, four piqué steps

√ Four piqué steps, four smooth steps

√ Four high steps, four forward crossed steps

√ Four rolled steps, four circle steps

√ Four long steps, four piqué steps

Perform all the steps joining one to the next.

Methods of correction related to the lack of mobility and rhythm during the travels

To improve these aspects the exercises must be coordinated and continuous. The end and the beginning of the elements must have a logical union with the intermediate traveling steps in order to avoid abrupt position changes, which can cause the movement to stop.

Exercises:

1) Start the elements using slow and very marked rhythms to make the execution of the different steps easier.

√ Increase the difficulty of the steps or travels

√ Use less marked, faster or different percussive rhythms

2) Perform a simple element (for example, arm swing), then travel with a waltz step and repeat it.

√ Perform a different travel each time (different type of steps)

√ Try more difficult exercises

Game

Objective: To develop the imagination, skill and rhythm with connecting exercises.

Exercise: Start with three or four gymnasts in a row. Each of them represents a different figure, for instance, a robot, a scarecrow, etc. and holds that figure while each person takes turns playing the game.

The rest of the girls listen to the melody, seated with their back to the row not to see their movements. They are waiting for their turn to perform traveling steps.

The girls stand up one at a time and perform each figure down the line. Move to the different figures using a different traveling step between each one.

The row of girls may be shifted if necessary.

The objectives of the game are to:

√ Stay in the line

√ Keep the exercises moving

√ Follow the rhythm of the music

√ Avoid repeating a traveling step (one out of three or four required)

√ Perform the exercises correctly

Variations:

√ Increase the number of gymnasts (the number of figures and travels to be performed will increase as well)

√ Execute complex traveling steps (combinations)

√ Use melodies with marked rhythm changes

Game

Objective: To develop the imagination, skill and rhythm with connecting exercises.

Exercise: Start with two rows of four girls each, facing each other. If the number of girls is high, the game can be played by teams. One row selects the figures, the other row makes an imitation of its partner. Alternate teams.

Two girls, one from each team, will perform the traveling steps through the other team, at the same time. Those two girls will then return to the row of the other team, taking the place of the other girl.

Traveling Steps Game

Points may be assigned as follows: correct performance of exercises and traveling steps — one point; originality — one point.

SWINGS AND CIRCUMDUCTIONS

In this group we must differentiate the following movements: swings, circumductions, waves and figure-eights.

Swings

Swings are a simple but important group of elements since they act as connections between elements. Swings provide smoothness and amplitude to the movements.

All swings can be done with one or two arms, starting the movement from the shoulders and keeping the arms stretched. Both arms can swing simultaneously, alternately or asymmetrically.

Swings can be performed in the following planes:

a) Frontal

b) Sagittal (front to back)

c) Horizontal

The circles can move:

√ From front to back

√ From back to front

√ Inward or outward

√ To the right or to the left

Watch whether the palm of the hand is facing up or down when finishing the movement.

a) <u>Frontal plane.</u>

Simultaneous

Alternating   Asymmetric

b) <u>Sagittal plane (front and back).</u>

Simultaneous   Alternating

Asymmetric

c) <u>Horizontal plane.</u>

Simultaneous   Alternating   Asymmetric

Circumductions

The center of the circles in circumductions with the arms is the shoulder.

With the arms straight, circumductions can be done in these planes:

a) Frontal plane

b) Sagittal plane

c) Horizontal plane

a) <u>Frontal plane.</u> Circumduction with one arm or both, alternating or asymmetrically.

Simultaneous   Alternating   Asymmetric

b) <u>Sagittal plane.</u> With one or two arms, simultaneously, alternating or asymmetrically.

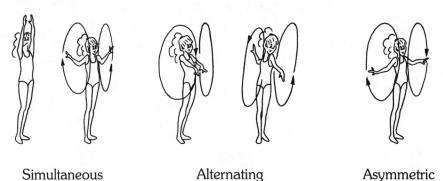

Simultaneous   Alternating   Asymmetric

c) <u>Horizontal plane.</u> With one or two arms, simultaneously, alternating or asymmetrically.

Simultaneous

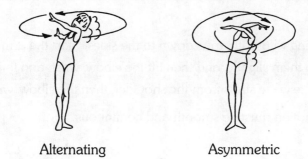

Alternating   Asymmetric

Combine small circles starting from the elbow with circumductions in all the planes, simultaneously or alternating.

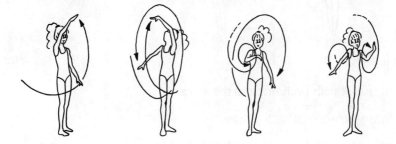

1) In the frontal plane do a circumduction with the right arm clockwise followed by the left arm counterclockwise. Next, draw a small circle with the right arm clockwise and finish with another small circle with the left arm counterclockwise. Both small and big circles are to be performed alternately.

2) Do a circumduction with the left arm forward, in the sagittal plane, and a small circle with the right arm in the same plane, simultaneously or alternating.

3) Do a horizontal circumduction with the right arm, and a small circle with the left arm, first in the same direction then in the opposite direction.

Waves

Begin standing with both arms down to the sides. Start the arm wave from the shoulders, lifting them slightly, and then lift the elbow, wrist, and finally the fingers. The descent of the wave starts from the shoulder, then the elbow, wrist and fingers.

The wave motion must be smooth and continuous.

Variations:

√ Do the wave with both arms to the sides

√ Do the wave alternating the arms

√ Do the wave with both arms in front of body

√ Do the wave in front of the body alternating the arms

√ Combine small waves with big waves

Figure-eights with arms

Begin standing, arms at sides, lifted slightly. Bend the elbows to draw an inward horizontal circle (under the arm) and then cross both arms in front at head height, lift and open them to the rear by doing a horizontal circumduction over the head, with a slight extension of the torso.

COMMON MISTAKES IN THE EXECUTION OF SWINGS AND METHODS OF CORRECTION

a) Stiff arms and contracted hands

b) Lack of amplitude in the movement

Method of correction for stiff arms and contracted hands

Arms should not be completely straight. A slightly curved arm is needed when executing these movements. The arms should not appear bent.

The hands, like the arms, are to be slightly curved in the direction of the movement.

Game

Exercise: Execute marches with arm swings and circumductions, with all movements tense to a maximum. Next, execute the same movements with the body relaxed.

Considering these two opposite states (tense and relaxed), we can find the one in between most suitable to our needs.

For these exercises we can use the following similes:

√ Robot-like movements for exercises in a tense state

√ Rag doll-like movements for exercises in a relaxed state

Method of correction for the lack of amplitude in the movement

It is necessary to develop the mobility of every joint as much as possible, since this allows all the movements to be performed easier and more confidently.

The radius of the swings or circumductions is as wide as possible, and should remain the same during the entire movement.

Game

Exercise: In pairs, one gymnast in front of the other, join hands. It is recommended to pair gymnasts of the same height.

Each gymnast will try to stretch further than her partner executing swings or circumductions, without moving the torso or lifting the feet from the floor.

Next, try the same exercise allowing movement of the trunk and lifting the heels.

On an erasable board, have the girls draw the movment of the arm, trying to make a circle as big as possible. The purpose of this exercise is for the girls to be aware of their movements. These movements should emphasize having great amplitude although sacrificing expression. Expressiveness will be highly considered later on.

Game

Objective: To give amplitude to the movements, improve individual coordination and develop the imagination.

Exercise: Perform the most swings, circumductions or other movements, and to stretch as far as possible.

Two gymnasts take a position facing each other, and perform exercises holding at least one of their hands (by the palm, the back of the hand or the fingers). The movements must have a large amplitude, touching the partner with only

one part of the body. It is required to keep at least one part of their body in contact. The gymnasts are free to perform turns, face each other, work back to back, to the sides, etc. The exercises are performed either in a specific area or around the whole gym.

It is recommended the girls take a few minutes to plan the movements. One of the girls guides the exercise while the other follows her (like a rock and roll partner dance) without losing contact.

The couple must remain in contact and keep the movement going.

The girls try to continue performing different elements as long as possible without mistakes.

TORSO MOVEMENTS AND WAVES (BODY WAVES)

Perhaps the most important difference between classical dance and rhythmic gymnastics is the movement of the torso. In ballet the object is to keep the torso and back straight. In rhythmic gymnastics, the composition of an exercise must include forward, side, and back body waves. The following preparatory exercises will improve this group of elements.

Preparatory Movements

a) Torso flexion.

1) Sitting, bend legs, knees apart and soles of feet together. Hands hold the ankles, bending the body forward and pushing the knees toward the floor.

2) Sitting, legs together and extended, stretch torso forward.

Stretch the torso, feet flexed, toes upward

Stretch the torso with feet pointed, toes forward.

3) Sitting, legs extended and open, stretch the torso.

Stretch torso to the side over one leg, chest against the knee. Stretch to the right and left with flexed feet.

Stretch torso over the leg trying to touch the leg with the side of the body. Keep the feet pointed (right and left).

Stretch torso forward, chest against floor.

Combine the three exercises.

b) <u>Torso extension.</u>

1) Kneeling, stretch upper torso backwards without moving the hips, hands to the floor. Balance the movement by stretching forward after each exercise.

Variations:

√ One leg stretched and the other bent. Place weight on bent knee . Stretch the torso until the hands reach the floor. Alternate legs.

√ One leg stretched and the other bent. Sit on the heel. Stretch the torso backwards until the hands reach the floor. Alternate legs.

Standing

Stand, face a barre and hold it at about waist height. Extend the torso, keeping the legs together.

Variations:

√ Move one leg forward, keeping the weight on leg in rear. Alternate legs

√ Move one leg backward, keeping the weight on the leg in front. Altermate legs

√ Repeat the three exercises without holding to the bars. Raise arms overhead to touch the floor with the hands

c) Side torso bend.

   1) Kneeling, one leg bent and the other stretched laterally, stretch torso toward the stretched leg. Alternate legs.

Variation:

  √ Stretch the torso toward the support leg with the knee on the floor.

   2) Stand, facing the barre. Shift weight onto one leg and stretch the torso laterally toward the other leg.

Variations:

  √ Perform the lateral flexion, holding the bar with the arm on the side of the flexion. The other arm accompanies the movement of the torso by stretching over the head. Alternate sides.

  √ Perform the lateral flexion without arm support. Stretch one arm over the head (the one opposite the flexion side) and curve the other arm at about waist height in front of the body.

  √ Perform the lateral flexion with legs together.

d) Circular motion of the torso.

 Legs slightly apart, both arms extended forward horizontally. Perform a circular motion of the torso as the body is stretched forward, to the right, backwards, and to the left. Alternate directions.

Variations:

√ At a 45° angle

√ At more than a 90° angle

e) Torso rotation.

 Stand with legs apart, arms extended to sides. Rotate the torso to the left and bend the body forward to touch the floor with right hand. Return to starting position and perform the rotation in the opposite direction.

Body Waves

Body waves are a valuable group of elements that should be included more often in the composition of any exercise. Waves are used as relaxation elements after quick and smooth movements. The movement is waving and continuous. The whole body is involved, and the movement is similar to a snake crawl.

a) <u>Body wave forward.</u> The movement of the body assimilates the imaginary push of a wave which moves up the rear of body. The wave starts from the feet, going through the knees, thighs, hips, torso, and neck, finishing with the head and arms. Progressions of body waves will be explained later on in the practice exercises.

It is possible to:

√ End on both legs

√ End on only one leg

Variations:

√ Kneeling with a rise to the tops of the toes (toe rise)

√ Finishing in a back scale balance, legs apart in a split position

b) <u>Backward body wave.</u> This is the same movement as in the forward body wave, but performed in the opposite direction. In this case the wave will descend the front of the body, by pushing it backwards slightly from the head, going through neck, shoulders, chest, abdomen and knees. The wave finishes with a bend of the knees. It can be performed by finishing on both feet or only on one of them.

c) Side body wave. This is like the forward body wave in its upward direction but this time the movement is done up the side of the body. The wave pushes from the feet, moving the body in the direction of the push and smoothly going through the knee, thigh, hip, side, shoulders, and head.

It can be performed:

√ With legs apart

√ Beginning with legs apart, and closing them to finish the body wave

√ With legs together

√ With a 360° turn, finishing with legs together

COMMON MISTAKES IN THE EXECUTION AND METHODS OF CORRECTION

a) Stiffness when bending

b) Lack of amplitude

c) Incomplete or short body wave

Methods of correction related to stiffness when bending

Objective: To gain enough flexibility to stretch to the horizontal.

Exercises: These can be done individually or in pairs, using stall bars.

Generally, the exercises in pairs caused a forced stretch with the help of the partner.

It is important after every stretch, and especially after a forced stretch of any joint, to compensate with stretches in the opposite direction.

Example: In pairs: one gymnast is on her hands and knees. The other one, kneeling at the side with her back to her partner, places her feet under her partner's abdomen and performs a backward bend of the torso resting on her partner's back. She then sits up and stretches forward.

Lift one leg, first with the knee bent then fully extended (alternate legs). Perform the side torso stretch in a similar way

Method of correction related to an incomplete and short wave

Every movement has to be continuous and finish with the head.

Exercise: Perform a torso flexion, look around and try to describe what is being seen. This will help to correct the head position.

Method of correction related to an incomplete and short wave

The wave has to be continuous, going from joint to joint without missing any of them.

Exercises:

a) Body wave forward.

1) Kneeling, move waist forward.

2) Stand, facing a barre or a wall, six inches away with arms at sides. Start with knees bent and touching the wall, keep heels on floor. Continue the wave by touching the wall with first the hip and then the abdomen.

3) Stand, arms stretched, and grasp barre at waist height. Perform the previous exercise without touching the barre. Continue the exercise by lifting the chest (torso extension) until reaching the starting position.

4) Stand sideways to the barre. One arm is stretched to the side, grasping the barre at waist height. The other arm is stretched forward, torso bent forward and knees slightly bent. The arm which is not holding the barre follows the wave motion. It starts to descend when moving the knees forward and it reaches the lower body when moving the waist forward. The arm begins its travel to the rear during the torso extension. Finally, perform the entire exercise rising up to the toes when moving the knees forward.

5) Legs in demi-plié, torso forward. Place the arms diagonally forward and downward, and shoulders upward. Perform the whole exercise without lifting the heels. Once this is done correctly, do it on the toes.

b) Side body wave.

1) Legs spread far apart, hands on hips, weight on left leg. The body is slightly bent to the right. Shift the weight to the right leg by bending the knees and shift the side torso bend to the left. The knees remain parallel to each other. Finish the body wave closing the left leg to the right.

2) Start from the same position as before, weight on left leg, sideways to a barre or wall (six inches away). Begin the previous movement touching the knee, thigh and hip to the barre and return to the starting position (repeat several times).

3) Stand with right side of body to the barre, weight on left leg, left hand grasping barre at waist height. With the right arm extended downward to the side, slowly lift the arm with elbow slightly higher than the hand. At the same time shift the weight from left side to right side, bending the knees and tilting the head to the left. The arm continues moving upward while lifting the torso (a side torso bend to the left will take place), and stretches to reach a vertical line. Perform the same movement to the left side.

4) Without support, perform the same movement. First, with only one weight shift, that is with the wave motion to only one side, and then to the right and to the left, without stopping.

Perform these exercises first without lifting the heels; then perform the body wave finishing on the toes.

BALANCES

The balance exercises require a support on a single part of the body such as the foot, knee or buttock muscles. The balance must be held long enough to prove control of the movement. Depending on the length of the balance, the grade of difficulty will be: middle — one second; superior — two seconds. Balances accentuate a theme of the music and provide beauty to the composition. The variety of balance elements is unlimited. We will select a broad view of this group of elements.

Balance on one leg

a) Support leg extended holding the other leg in different positions: front, side and back. Depending on the position of the free leg, we will have the following variations:

√ Bent leg front, side and back

√ Flexed leg front, side and back

√ Extended leg front, side and back

b) Support leg bent and the other leg in different positions front, side and back.

√ Free leg bent front, side and back.

√ Free leg flexed front, side and back.

√ Free leg extended front, side and back.

c) <u>Lunge Scale.</u> Legs apart, one extended and the other bent, weight on bent leg.

√ Lunge forward

√ Lunge sideward

√ Lunge backward

d) <u>Back scale balance.</u> On one leg, lift the other leg to the horizontal line while bending the torso backward. Arm positions may vary, but the simplest way is with the arms stretched overhead (reaching toward the floor).

When learning this exercise, it is recommended to practice standing sideways to a barre or wall. For example: standing with the left side to the barre, grasp barre with left hand, right arm stretched up to the vertical line, take one step forward with left leg. Lift the right leg while bending the torso backward, first reaching back with the right arm until it touches the floor.

Perform the same exercise without support.

e) <u>Front scale, back scale.</u> Balance on left leg and lift right leg to the rear above the horizontal, arms up on both sides of the head. Hold this position for one second, then turn the body to the right, keeping the right leg up. Perform a back scale or back scale balance and return to standing position. Alternate legs.

f) <u>Balance on left leg, lift right leg to a flexed position in front of the body up to 90°</u> <u>or higher.</u> Hold this balance for two seconds. Rotate body to the left, keeping the right leg up. The right leg finished behind the body at 90^0 or higher.

g) <u>Balance on one leg.</u> Lift free leg extended in front of the body. Move leg from front to back without dropping the leg below horizontal. Alternate legs. As a variation do this exercise on half toes.

h) <u>Balance on one leg.</u> Hold the free leg with one or two hands and perform a vertical split to the front, side or back.

Variations:

√ Perform the balance without support of the hands

√ Do the exercise on half toe

Balance on Knees

Stretch the left leg behind the body without touching the floor, arms to the sides.

Balance on Buttock Muscles

Without arm support, extend the legs without touching the floor.

Variations:

√ Balance with legs bent

√ Balance with one leg bent, the other stretched

COMMON MISTAKES IN THE EXECUTION OF BALANCES AND METHODS OF CORRECTION

a) Loss of balance, causing any part of the body or apparatus to touch the floor, or the execution of supplementary movements in order to avoid falling and to regain the position.

b) Execution of a supplementary step during the performance of a balance element (foot, knee or buttock muscles).

Methods of correction related to the general loss of balance

The whole body must achieve proper muscle tension in order to control the impulses and shifts of the center of gravity.

1) Balance without displacement.

Exercises: Perform the basic balance elements on the floor, making them more complex when mastered.

Perform arm movements in all directions and combine with torso bending:

√ On toes

√ On one foot (heel on floor)

√ Lift leg, flexed (to the front, to the rear)

√ Lift leg, extended (to the front, to the rear)

√ On one knee

√ Without leg support (on buttock muscles)

If balance if lost, restart the element until the proper time is achieved (2 seconds). The balance time for each gymnast must be measured in real time; that is, for one second we will count 101, for 2 seconds 102, and so on.

2) Balances with traveling steps.

It is important to keep your bearing and to maintain correct posture during the traveling steps.

Exercises:

√ March steps: slow and fast

√ Jumps and short jumps: change the position of the legs when performing the jumps

√ Stop:

    • on both feet   • on one foot

    • on the heels   • on the toes

√ Alter the body positions.

√ Alter the support point from the previous traveling step.

√ Travel:

    • on a line on the floor   • over stacked mats

        • up and down inclined mats

√ Perform different elements with these traveling steps.

Methods of correction related to the execution of a supplementary step during the performance of an element of balance

Proper muscular tension is required during balance elements. It is very important to step far out with the leg extended in order to achieve a correct line of balance.

In the general physical preparation, it is important to strengthen all of the muscles working against gravity. This will help with control of the balances in all positions.

Exercise: Hold a balance using the following parts of the body:

√ Right knee and left hand fingers

√ Buttock muscles and one foot (the other leg stretched or bent)

√ One elbow and both knees

√ Right hand and foot

√ Buttock muscles and one hand

√ Shift the number of support points

√ Use all the positions of stretched, prone, supine, sideways, etc.

Game

Objective: To improve balance in the gymnasts. To strengthen creativity by searching for new balance positions.

Balance Game

Exercise: While music is playing the coach tells the gymnasts to move freely around the gym. Suddenly, the coach stops the music for five seconds. The gymnasts have to stop and hold the posture they had when the music was stopped. They must remain in that posture until the music starts again. During each silence the gymnasts must adopt a different posture.

The girls must avoid using support to save them from falling and avoid moving during the silence. The gymnasts are not allowed to repeat their static position.

Variations:

√ Designate the position in which the girls remain stopped during the silence

√ See who create new and original positions

TURNS AND ROTATIONS

Turns are basic elements in the composition of an exercise. They are the most difficult group of elements. They can be performed on the buttock muscles, back, on one or two feet, in the air combined with jumps; directly initiated on the toes (relevé) or going through demi-plié up to relevé (spring action).

The direction of the rotation can be outward, when the turn is performed in the direction of the free leg, or inward when the turn is performed toward the support leg. The positions of the arms, legs, and body will vary, but during the turn the support point on the floor must remain stationary. The movements are: half turn (180°), single turn (360°), turn and half (540°), and double turn (720°). The last three turns are of high difficulty. Before performing the turn, we must focus the sight on a spot in order to execute the turns correctly. Begin the movement, keeping the head fixed, while the body turns as much as it can. Continue to turn the body and snap the head around quickly to find the spot. By doing this we will avoid dizziness. It is important to step into the turn with the supporting leg. This step completes 1/4 of the turn and facilitates the rest of the turn.

There are many kind of turns that can be performed. All the balance positions previously mentioned can be performed as turns.

Types:

√ With step   √ Spring action

√ Shifting legs   √ Dropping to floor

√ Ending with balance   √ With travel steps

√ Jumping

Changing the position of the leg while turning increases the difficulty.

Turns from Standing Position

Perform two steps turning, step 1/2 turn, step 1/2 turn, holding second position with the legs and arms. Spot to the right when turning to the right, and to the left when turning to the left. Turn without changing the separation of the legs, shifting the weight onto each leg.

Variations:

    √ Perform a series of consecutive turns (chainé turns)

    √ In the same starting position as the previous exercise, turn faster and close the legs after the side step. When stepping, the arms are held in second position. We will look for the spot, turn and quickly regain the spot

Preparatory exercises for the turn

Perform a half turn in:

    √ 4 counts

    √ 2 counts

    √ 1 count

Perform one complete turn in:

    √ 8 counts

    √ 4 counts

    √ 2 counts

    √ 1 count

a) <u>Turn with support leg extended and the other leg bent</u>: front, side, back

b) <u>Turn with support leg extended and the free leg extended</u>: front, side, back

c) <u>Turn with support leg extended and the other leg flexed</u>: front, side, back

d) <u>Turn with support leg bent, the other leg bent, flexed, and extended</u>: front, side, back

    Perform turns a) through d) rotating both inward and outward.

e) <u>Perform a turn finishing on the floor</u>. Stand on one leg with the other leg stretched behind the body and perform a 360-degree turn. To finish the turn bend the support leg so the free leg can step on the floor, either behind or in front of the body.

> Continue with another movement:
>
> √ Go through a sitting position
>
> √ Continue through a stretched position
>
> √ Stand up again

f) <u>Squat and perform a turn followed by a roll</u>.

g) <u>Illusion to inside of support leg</u>. Stretch arms overhead, left leg slightly forward. Lift leg slightly forward and then kick to the rear and upward, while bending the arms and body toward the floor (close to right leg). Execute the turn when the body and left leg are in a vertical line, then lift the body and lower the leg.

h) <u>Turn with spring</u>. On the landing of a split leap, spring up into a turn and finish with balance.

Kneeling Turn

Kneel on the left leg, right leg bent in front of body with toes on the floor, arms stretched to the sides. Turn $180°$ to the left, closing the knees together. Turn another $180°$ keeping the left foot fixed. Finish the exercise on right knee, left leg bent in front of body.

Variations:

> √ $360°$ turn on one knee.

√ From a kneeling position, stand with a 360⁰ turn. Begin with the left knee on floor, right knee bent forward, foot on floor. Shift weight onto the right leg and turn to the left as the body straightens up.

360-degree Turn on Buttock Muscles

Turn with legs:

√ Bent

√ Stretched

√ One leg bent, one leg extended

Spin on Back

This spin has been widely used in break-dancing. Sitting with the legs stretched, place left hand on the floor. With the right arm and leg, push to spin to the left, while bringing the body to the rear and bending the legs and knees toward the chest.

Variation:

√ Spin on back with circle of the legs. Laying supine with legs stretched and close together, move right leg to the left drawing a large horizontal circle. When this leg reaches the head, start with left leg. When the left leg reaches the head, the right leg reaches the initial position. In order to perform the spin, thrust right leg to the left, turning the body toward the right, and follow the movement of the legs as previously mentioned.

COMMON MISTAKES IN THE EXECUTION OF TURNS AND METHODS OF CORRECTION

a) Insufficient elevation of the heel

b) Placing the heel on the floor when turning

c) Little hops while turning

Methods of correction related to insufficient elevation the heel

The ankle must be fully stretched, having the heel vertically as far from the floor as possible.

Exercise: Stand, facing the wall or barre, and raise the heel keeping the balance on half toe. Execute the turns with hands grasping the bars.

Perform:

√ Little stepping turns without bending the torso and with torso flexion

√ Turns with hands off the bar, placing them back on the bar when the turn is completed

Perform these turns:

√ On one or two feet and knees bent or stretched

√ With the help of a partner

√ Without help

Methods of correction related to placing the heel on the floor when turning

This problem can be caused by an incorrect foot position, inward rotation of the toe and knee, or by having the center of gravity misplaced, causing a loss of balance.

Exercise: Correct the position of the foot while holding onto the barre. Decrease the size of the possible movements when turning, by using: a hoop, stacked mats, a line on the floor, a spot on the floor.

Perform the turns by holding a rope suspended from the ceiling or with the help of a partner marking the axis of the turn.

Methods of correction related to little hops when turning

Hops are caused by the lack of or the excess of impulse given to the step when beginning the turn.

Exercise: Begin the exercise with a balanced turn of 45°, then one of 90°, one complete turn, and two complete turns. The thrust of the arms will progressively increase in order to increase the degrees of the turn. Always begin with a step to the side. To realize the amount of strength needed to perform each turn, alternate strong impulses with light ones.

Game

Objective: Keep the center of gravity fixed when spinning perpendicular to the floor (on a vertical axis).

Pivot Game

Exercise: One gymnast performs a turn inside a hoop. The hoop is held by a partner at waist height. The gymnast performing the turn will try not to touch the hoop or bend the body.

The goal is to perform as many turns to the right or to the left without touching the hoop as possible.

√ Turn with both feet on the ground

√ Turn both directions

√ Change the position of the free leg

√ Change the position of the support leg

JUMPS & LEAPS

Jumps and leaps are a very important group of elements because they provide a sense of amplitude, lightness and dynamism.

They can be done from one or both feet to finish on one or both feet as well. It is always required to bend the legs a little when landing. This allows us to absorb the shock. During the jump, the legs must show as much amplitude of movement as possible.

The positions of the arms may vary.

Preparatory jumps

These exercises are to be performed first with the help of a ballet barre and then
  without.

a) Jump eight times in each one of the positions, first, second and fifth, keeping
     the body stretched as well as the legs and ankles.

b) In fifth position, jump with changes of the feet in the air.

c) Perform 4, 6, 8 or more little jumps alternating first, second and fifth positions.

Jumps and Landings Using Both Feet Simultaneously

a) <u>Jump with extension of the body (arch jump)</u>.

Cat Jump

  √ Stretched legs

  √ Bent legs

b) <u>Jump and bring legs toward the chest (tuck jump)</u>.

c) <u>Cat jump</u>.

d) <u>Pike jump</u>.

Stag Jump

Split Jump

  √ Legs open

  √ Legs together

e) <u>Split jump (both legs)</u>.

f) <u>Stag jump</u>.

g) <u>Double stag jump</u>.

h) <u>Ring jump</u>.

Double Stag Jump

Ring Jump

Jumps From One Foot Landing on One or Two Feet

a) <u>Hops on alternating legs, lifting free leg to a bent position</u>.

  Variation:

  √ Lift free leg to horizontal

b) <u>Scissors</u>.

Forward, arms stretched. Step forward with the right foot and kick left leg into the air. When left leg is in the air, jump and switch legs to kick right leg into the air, landing first on left foot and then closing right to left.

Scissors backward. Step on left foot, kick right leg to the rear. Jump and immediately switch legs to kick left leg into the air, landing first on right leg and then closing left to right.

Variations:

√ Begin the scissors with the opposite leg

√ Perform, alternately, a forward scissors and a backward scissors

√ While performing a backward scissors, bend the second leg and arch the back

c) <u>Cat leap</u>. Similar to a scissors but with the legs bent. During the preparation of the jump, swing both arms up over the head to assist the push.

Variations:

√ Half turn (180°) during cat leap.

√ One whole turn (360°) during cat leap.

d) <u>Tuck jump</u>. Chassé with left leg. Lift right knee to the chest, then join left leg to the right in the air. Land on both feet simultaneously, arms stretched to the sides, swinging them up over the head on the take-off.

Variations:

√ Half turn (180°) during tuck jump

√ One whole turn (360°) during tuck jump

e) <u>Cabriole jump</u>. Kick right leg forward, push off the left leg and beat tthe left leg to the right in the air, landing on one or both feet.

Variations:

√ Cabriole to the right and to the left

√ Cabriole forward and backward

√ Combine the four different directions

f) Open hop to the right and to the left. Step forward oblique with right leg and hop on this leg, throwing left leg backward to achieve almost a split position. Repeat to the left.

g) Split leap. Leap from one foot to the other, positioning the legs in a split during the flight. Chassé forward with left leg, thrust right leg forward to leap and land on the right. During the leap, one arm forward (opposite the front leg) and the other to the back. Perform leaps with both legs.

Progressions:

√ Perform leaps considering their length (leap from one line to another at a far distance)

√ Perform leaps considering their height (leaps over obstacles)

√ Combine length and height

Variations:

√ Bend the back leg and perform a torso extension when during the leap

√ Bend the front leg to begin the jump and extend it during the flight

h) Side leap. Side chassé with left leg, turn 180° left to thrust right leg in the direction of the movement. Follow with a kick of the left leg to the opposite direction. Show legs in side split during the flight, landing on right leg.

Variation:

√ Perform a side leap making a 90° turn when landing.

i) Turning leap. Chassé with right leg. Step across with left leg making a half turn to the right. Finish the turn right throwing the right leg forward into the air and performing a leap. (Legs open to a split)

Variations:

√ Bend back leg during the leap, arching the back

√ Perform a series of turning leaps, one with the leg extended and the other with the leg bent

j) <u>Double stag leap with chassé</u>. Chassé with left leg, thrust right leg forward. While in the air bend right leg and thrust left leg to the rear. Stretch arms to the sides during the chassé, swinging them forward and upward on take-off.

Variations:

√ Bend left leg during the jump

√ Stretch both legs during the jump to finish in an open split

k) <u>Gazelle leap with take-off similar to the previous leap, but extending the front leg during the flight</u>.

l) <u>Fouetté</u>. This jump is the preparation for the Tour Jeté. Step with right leg, kick left leg forward into the air to hold it at horizontal. Perform a half turn during the jump, landing on the right leg. Stretch arms upward during the jump in order to keep the body straight. Alternate legs.

m) <u>Tour Jeté</u>. Chassé with left leg, kick right leg forward into the air. Perform a half turn to the left and execute back scissors by kicking left leg back. Land on right leg. The arms must swing overhead on takeoff and remain in this position to keep the torso straight. The arms lower on the landing.

n) <u>Single leg leap</u>. Chassé with right leg, kick left forward and hold it at horizontal. Perform a half turn left, jumping with the right leg over the left leg to land on right leg. Hold left leg in position.

o) <u>Split leap with change of legs extended (switch leap)</u>. Chassé with left leg, thrust right leg forward. While in the air, swing right leg extended to the rear while simultaneously swinging left leg forward. Finish the exercise in split, arms as in the split leap. Repeat with the other leg.

Variation:

√ Bend the back leg and arch the back when legs are open in split.

Note: Combine different or same leaps to make a series with intermediate chassés or stepping to shift the impulse leg. The combination of different leaps increases the difficulty.

COMMON MISTAKES IN THE EXECUTION OF JUMPS AND LEAPS AND METHODS OF CORRECTION

    a) Little elevation when jumping

    b) Lack of amplitude while in the air

    c) Lack of shock absorption when landing

Methods of correction related to little elevation in the leaps

This can be caused by a lack of coordination between arms and legs a lack of flexibility of the lower body. It is necessary to perform exercises to improve this coordination. It is also important to design a specific physical preparation program to increase the power of the legs.

Exercises: Perform many kinds of jumps/leaps assisting with the arms on takeoff.

√ Vertical and longitudinal jumps/leaps

√ With the legs bent or flexed (maximum flexion)

√ With one or two legs

√ Leaps over obstacles:

    • From a lower to higher height

    • From a shorter to longer length, increasing both, height and length

√ Increase the number of leaps

Method of correction related to a lack of amplitude during the leap

Increasing the amount of time spent in the air (airtime) will allow a larger split and elasticity during the exercises.

Exercise: Perform leaps with different movements:

√ 45-degree, 90-degree and 180-degree turns

√ Stretch or bend one or both legs during the flight

√ Touch, push or press a ball or similar object situated to a certain height (increase the height)

Method of correction related to the lack of shock absorption when landing

The first point of contact with the floor after the flight is the toe. Then the heel is lowered to the floor and the leg bends. This progression helps to avoid noise and abruptness on the landing, making the exercise smoother and easier.

Exercises: Practice jumping down from a certain height:

√ Onto a mat

√ Onto the floor

√ Onto one or both feet

√ Increase the height of the jump

√ Initiate another jump immediately after the landing and vary:

• The height

• The direction

• The difficulty of the obstacle

• The difficulty of the following element to be performed

Game

Objective: improve coordination, height, and airtime of the jumps/leaps.

Who can perform more leaps in a row reaching a predetermined goal?

Variations:

√ Perform a different element each time

√ Increase the height, length or both of the object to be surpassed (rope, bench, partner, etc.)

Airtime-Improvement Game

√   Touch, push or catch an object at a greater height

Note: End the game when the landings become noisy and abrupt.

PRE-ACROBATICS

This is not a required group of elements for floor exercise, but pre-acrobatics provide colorfulness to the composition and help develop important skills. Typical tumbling elements are not allowed in rhythmic gymnastics. Several examples of pre-acrobatic elements will be mentioned, divided into five groups:

√ Rolls

√ Splits (front, side)

√ Supports on one or both hands

√ Horizontal supports

√ Bridges and walkovers

Rolls

a) Forward rolls with no flight.

√ With both hands

√ Without hands

√ On one shoulder

b) Backwards.

√ Over both shoulders with hands

√ Over one shoulder

c) Side roll. This type of roll is not considered a pre-acrobatic move, but it has been included in this group because it is a type of roll.

Tuck knees to the chest with   Extended legs open to sides with

√ Arms up   √ Arms up

√ Arms down   √ Arms down

  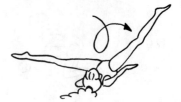

Side rolls can be performed from a standing position. Lower the body by bending the legs, place one shoulder on the ground, roll to the other one, sit up on the knee and return to starting position.

Splits

It is permissible to pass through a split without stopping.

Split front   Split side

Variations: Perform a front split, bringing the chest to the knee of the front leg. Holding the foot with both hands, roll over to the back keeping legs apart and continue rolling back to the split.

From a split, lean forward and then pull backwards, finishing on the knee of the back leg with the other leg stretched forward.

Temporary Support on One or Both Hands

Lift both legs without stopping and without reaching a vertical line. Support on the forearms is not allowed.

Variations with support on both hands:

√ Support on both hands, lift both legs at the same time.

√ Kick legs alternately to perform a scissors.

Variations with Support on one Hand

Begin kneeling and lean forward on right arm. Swing the left arm while kicking back with the left leg. Lift the hips, legs apart, to perform a double scissors, landing on the right leg.

a) Acro jump. Sit with the right leg bent and left leg extended. Use left arm for support on the floor and right arm free. Swing the right arm and throw the left leg into the air; at the same time lift the hips and arch the back slightly. Extend both legs during the flight, landing first on the left leg, from the toe to the knee, then on the right leg. The element travels diagonally to the right and to the rear.

b) <u>Cheststand</u>. From the knees, roll forward on the body with the hips forward to a support on the chest with the legs lifted overhead. The arms can be over the head or alongside the body.

Cheststand

Variations:

√ Kick one leg forward to end in a split

√ Kick one leg forward and perform a scissors with both legs

c) <u>Fish flop</u>. From a seated position, lift both legs to the vertical line while rolling the body backwards. Continue the elevation of the legs and torso up to the vertical. Support with the right shoulder while passing through the vertical. Lift the chest forward and lower the body by rolling over the chest, hip and knee.

Cheststand Variation

Variation:

√ After passing through the vertical, split legs while the body is lowered

d) <u>Bridge</u>. From a position lying on back, place hands by shoulders and bend knees so that feet are on floor. Extend the arms and knees to push off the floor. It is important that the shoulders are over the hands.

e) Back walkover.

f) Front walkover.

COMMON MISTAKES IN THE EXECUTION OF THE PRE-ACROBATICS AND METHODS OF CORRECTION

Back walkover with hoop

a) Stopping in a position.

b) Small amplitude in general.

Methods of correction related to stopping in a position

In pre-acrobatic elements the position is to be marked but is not to remain static. Avoid practicing the pre-acrobatic skills alone. Try to introduce another exercise right after it so that the gymnast will not find herself static during the pre-acrobatic.

Exercises:

1) Begin standing, perform a pre-acrobatic, return to standing position, and repeat it.

2) Jump or climb over an object, causing a change of position.

3) Draw lines on the floor and try to reach them.

> *Example:* Perform a support move on both hands on one side of stacked mats, jump over the mats and perform the support on the other side. This can

also be done with support on one side of the mats, on the top of the mats, and then on the other side.

4) Throw a ball and catch it after the pre-acrobatic.

Example: throw the ball, do a side roll, catch the ball. Throw it again and roll again.

Method of correction related to a lack of amplitude

The element is not totally finished and is cut off before it is completed. The causes may vary depending on how one element or another is treated. These causes can be lack of flight, lack of flexibility, lack of strength during the support on hands or incorrect roll technique.

Generally, especially when working with equipment, the necessity of catching it before it touches the floor forces the gymnast to make the movement shorter.

Game

Objective: To develop dynamism, speed and agility during the execution of the pre-acrobatics.

Exercise: The gymnasts are in a row, three feet apart from each other. The game consists of reaching an established point by rolling forward with the support of both hands.

Variations:

√ Roll forward with one hand

√ Roll forward without hands

√ Side roll, legs bent

√ Side roll, legs stretched and apart

√ Backwards roll with both hands

√ Backwards roll over one shoulder

In the pre-acrobatics with one or two support points where it is necessary to lift the hips and legs, place an object so that the gymnast can try to touch it each time she performs the element.

Rolling Game

Support with both hands:

√ One leg

√ Two legs

Support with one hand:

√ One leg

√ Scissors

√ Acro jump

Try to reach the highest point relative to the gymnast's height.

Note: When two or more elements (same or different) are executed consecutively, the series of elements increases the difficulty of execution. Example: series of leaps without intermediate steps.

Note: Any body difficulty performed with no relation to the equipment is not considered a difficulty.

MUSICAL ACCOMPANIMENT

Floor exercises can be adapted to any kind of musical rhythm. In this case the rhythm may be totally and exclusively selected to fit the style of the gymnast.

With respect to the slow and fast parts, a melody can be adapted to a gymnast with wide, slow and expressive movements. Likewise, lively, strong and fast music can be adapted to a fast and dynamic gymnast. The relaxed parts of the music have to be respected and should be used to give the gymnast a break or to perform wide movements such as waves, large stretching, etc. These elements must always appear in the composition of any exercise. Fast rhythms are suitable for leaps, turns, short runs, etc.

Chapter Two
Rope

Rope is the oldest of the five apparatus that constitute rhythmic gymnastics. It was first performed at the World Championships in Copenhagen in 1967. This apparatus might seem, from the point of view of the spectator, not very picturesque or spectacular. On the other hand, from the technical point of view, it is very important because its special handling requires complete physical preparation of the gymnast.

The technique of the rope has been developed based on the perfect control of its continuous movement. The movement can be done with a very fast rhythm or with a slow rhythm while the gymnast moves around the floor.

CHARACTERISTICS AND RULES OF THE APPARATUS

The material of the rope, according to the International Gymnastic Federation (F.I.G.), can be hemp or a synthetic plastic. The ropes made of synthetic plastic must possess the qualities of lightness and flexibility the same as those made out of hemp.

The length of the rope varies according to the height of the gymnast. To find the right length, use the following method: Hold both ends of the rope at shoulder height, with the center of the rope touching the floor.

The rope may not have handles at the ends, but a knot at each end is permissible. The ends can also be covered by an anti-slip material with a maximum length of 10 cm.

The diameter of the rope must be uniform. It can be reinforced in the center as long as the same material is used.

The rope must be a color

Rope and ball are the most recommended apparatus for introducing girls into the techniques of handling equipment. This is because girls usually play rope-jumping and others games so they are already familiar with the apparatus.

The rope is used in its full length or folded in parts: in 2 parts (doubled), in 3 parts (tripled), or in 4 parts (quadrupled). The rope ends are held with the thumb and index finger and can be held with one end in each hand or both ends in one hand.

If the exercises are executed with good technique, the rope will not deviate from or break its shape.

ELEMENTS OF THE BASIC TECHNIQUE

There are two basic rope movements, depending on the strength and speed applied: wide, slow movements and short, fast movements.

Combinations of fast and slow movements increase the difficulty. The rope must always be taut (not broken). If the tension is lost, it is due to bad coordination between the strength applied to move the rope and the movement of the body itself.

In order to perform little jumps, the body must keep a straight and tight position. The feet must push on the floor, stretching through the toe. The knees are stretched from the beginning of the jump, and bend slightly to land on the floor.

With the arms extended and slightly away from the body, the wrist produces the movement of the rope.

During the swings, the rope must be smoothly driven without touching the floor or any other part of the body, except when a wrap element is to be performed. During leaps with rope, the movement starts from the shoulders and then from the wrist. If during the leap the rope hits the floor, it is due to the lack of coordination between the rope circle and the leap. If the rope hits the toes (pointed toes), it is because the arms are bent.

Following are some of the movements executed with the rope:

√ Circular motions: Swings, circles and figure-eights

√ Little jumps

√ Leaps

√ Tosses

√ Wraps of the rope

√ Balance movements with the rope

CIRCULAR MOVEMENTS
Swings, circles, circumductions and figure-eights.

This group of elements, characterized as circular movements, requires good coordination between the movements of the rope and movements of the body. The initial position of the arms varies according to the type of elements- swings, circles or figure-eights. During figure-eights, the movement commences from the shoulder to the elbow and wrist; while for circles with the rope, the movement commences from the wrists and fingers.

Movements can be done with the rope stretched or folded in two, three or four parts. The rope may be held with one or two hands, at the ends or at the center, with the rope folded or stretched.

Movements can be done in the following planes:

Horizontal

√ Over the head

√ Around the body

√ Around the legs

Frontal

√ In front of the body

√ Behind of the body

Sagittal

√ To the right of the body

√ To the left of the body

This group of elements must show a contrast between fast and slow movements and exchanges of the rope from one hand to the other during the exercises.

Rope Swings

Swings are simple movements that can be used as connecting elements between other elements of higher difficulty. They are elements of great importance because they are part of the base technique of the rope. The rope must be always driven, it never goes by itself.

a) <u>Swings in the frontal plane.</u> Arms stretched and apart, rope open with one end in each hand. Commence the rope swing from the body and move the rope smoothly.

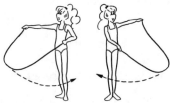

Variations:

√ Legs apart, bend right leg as the rope swings to the right; bend left leg as the rope swings to the left

√ Travel with two or three rhythmic steps to the right or to the left. This can be done in the same or the opposite direction of the swing

√ Combine the swing with a waltz step

√ Swing the rope to the right and step over the rope with the right leg then the left, ending with the rope behind the body. Swing the rope to the left and the right. When the rope swings back to the left, step back over the rope with the left leg then the right

√ The same exercise stepping over the rope to the front and back, without swings in between

√ One arm in front of the body, the other one behind. Swing from the right to the left and jump over the rope

b) <u>Swings in the sagittal plane.</u> Arms stretched and open to one side of the body. Swing forward and backward, on each side of the body.

1) Combine with two or three rhythmic steps, as many forward as backward.

2) Combine swing with a waltz step.

3) Swing rope in a lateral plane, forward and backward, jumping over the rope with one foot or with legs together and extended

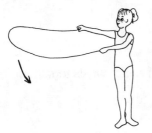  

4) Hold rope at the center (folded in two parts), swing it keeping the ends parallel.

c) <u>Swings in the horizontal plane.</u> Hold rope open, one end in each hand, left arm over the head and right arm below hip level to the left side.

Stand with weight on left leg. Swing rope from left to right and kick right leg forward into the rope. Continue the movement of the rope around behind the body. Kick left leg forward out of the rope as it returns to the front of the body.

Change direction of the rope.

Variations:

√   Rope open and arms extended, the left arm stretched vertically and to the right, right arm down to the side. Swing rope from back to front and from right to left, jump with legs together into the rope. Change direction of the rope.

√   Same initial position as the previous exercise. As the rope swing begins, place right hand on the floor and lift legs to pass through the rope. Perform two jumps in a row.

Rope Circles

Circles performed with the rope begin exclusively with movement of the wrist. They can be done either with one end of the rope in each hand with the hands together, or folded in 2, 3 or 4 parts with both ends in one hand.

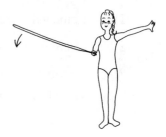

a) Circles in the frontal plane.

    1) Arms extended, one end of the rope in each hand, wrists together.

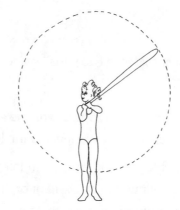

These circles can be combined with other elements:

√ Perform a side chassé while circling the rope (both directions)

√ Hold a balance while circling

√ Perform a side body wave with the circles

√ Repeat the previous element holding the rope with only one hand

√ With one hand only, perform a side leap with the circles

    2) Hold one end of the rope in one hand, and with the other hand hold the rope at its center. Perform circles in front of and behind the body in both directions. Alternate hands.

Combine the circles with other elements such as:

√ Side body wave. Catch the free end when finishing the body wave, ending with the rope folded in two parts

√ Circles with chassé. Catch the free end over the head during a jump

b) Circles in the sagittal plane.

1) One end of the rope in each hand with hands together. Perform circles forward and backward to the right and left sides of the body. Alternate, right-left.

Possible combinations:

√ Perform a waltz step with circles

√ Perform a side balance with circles

√ Perform various split leaps with circles

√ Perform a double stag jump

√ Repeat the elements mentioned above with both ends of the rope held in one hand

2) Rope folded in two parts. Hold both ends in one hand, and hold the center of the rope with the other hand. Perform circles forward and backward. Change hands.

Variations:

√ Perform small hops on one leg holding the other leg at the knee in passé

√ Hold a balance with circles of the rope

c) Circles in the horizontal plane.

1) Extend arms vertically upwards, one end of the rope in each hand with wrists together. Circle the rope in both directions.

2) Extend one arm up with both ends of the rope in one hand. Circle the rope in both directions.

Combine this movement with other elements. For example:

√ Perform a body wave forward ending in a balance

√ Lower to knees over the toes and execute a toe rise

√ Perform a chassé and jump from the gallop group (such as scissors)

√ Slide to a split followed by a seat spin

√ Repeat the previous elements with both ends of the rope held in one hand

3) With the rope folded in two parts, hold both ends in one hand and with the other hand hold the center. Draw circles over the head in both directions.

Combine with:

√ 360° turn, ending with the rope folded in 4 parts by catching the free end

√ Lower to knees over the toes with circles, then catch the free end and execute a side bend of the torso.

d) Circles exchanging the rope from one hand to the other.

1) Sagittal plane. Circle the rope and change hands while circling. Start with both ends in right hand. Stretch arms to the front and begin circles forward to the right side. On the third circle turn the body 90° to the left, placing the right arm behind the body (back of the hand facing upwards). Exchange the rope to the left hand while turning the body another 90° to the left, ending with the left arm at the front circling the rope. Alternate hands and directions.

Combine with:

√ Turn on one leg

√ Chassé during the first two circles of the rope, followed by a step to begin the turn

√ Cat leap with a 180° turn, exchanging rope from one hand to the other

2) Frontal plane. Circle rope and exchange hands. Start holding both ends held in left hand and perform circles to the right (counterclockwise). Kick right leg forward and exchange the rope to the right hand under the leg. Exchange hands again overhead.

Variations:

√ Perform exchange during a leap

√ Perform exchange with scissors

3) Horizontal plane. Perform circles with exchange. Begin holding both ends in one hand. Perform circles to the right and to the left at different heights, exchanging hands.

Possible combinations:

√ Perform circles at ankle height by exchanging the rope from hand to hand in front of and behind the legs

√ Perform an illusion exchanging the rope behind the support knee

√ Perform circles at waist height, exchanging hands in front of and behind the body

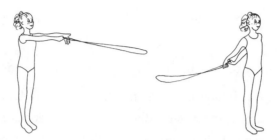

√ Perform turns with the body with exchanges in standing and kneeling positions

√ Perform the same exchanges at neck height

√ Perform the exchange during a seated spin, exchanging under the legs

√ Lying in a supine position, perform mills with the legs and exchange the rope from hand to hand when the leg is lifted

Circumductions

This movement starts from the shoulder and is accompanied by movement of the torso. The center of the circle drawn by the rope is the shoulder.

a) Circumductions in the frontal plane. Hold one end of the rope in each hand with the hands apart from each other at shoulder width. Circle the rope as wide as possible with arms stretched in both directions.

One possible combination is to perform the circumduction with a side chassé. Perform one large counterclockwise circumduction with chassé to the right. Finish with a smooth swing and begin the same exercise to the left.

b) <u>Circumduction in the horizontal plane.</u> Circle rope along with the torso, one end of the rope in each hand. Stand with legs apart, weight on flexed right leg. Move rope and torso to the right with a side bend, then continue to the rear with an arch of the torso. Shift the weight to both legs and continue moving weight to the left leg as the rope and torso move to the left. Shift weight back to both legs, bending torso forward slightly to return to the initial position.

Perform the same exercise with both ends of the rope in one hand, kneeling and moving to the sides, front and rear as far as possible (perform the circumductions in both directions and with both hands). The rope may be held with both hands or folded in three or four parts.

1) Large circumduction in the horizontal plane with side body roll. Start with the rope at the left side of the body and one end in each hand, hands apart. Sit with the legs extended and together. Swing the extended arms to the right, letting the body roll onto the right side while turning on the hip. Without touching the floor with the chest, continue the roll and return to the initial position.

The rope must not touch the floor, so the movement of the body has to be continuous. Perform the movement in both directions.

The same exercise can be done holding the rope in one hand. The rope is held with the right hand when the roll is to the right, and with the left hand when the rolls to the left. The rope may also be folded in three or four parts.

2) Horizontal circumduction around the body. Hold rope open to the right side, one end in each hand.

Start with the left arm stretched over the head, right arm extended at approximately hip height. Swing rope to left as the right hand moves up to shoulder height, both shoulders facing forward. Continue circle to the left, lifting right arm over the head, and lowering the left arm to hip height. When the circle reaches the back, both arms move to an equal height and then return to initial position. Change directions.

Variations:

√ Execute circumduction while turning the body

√ Perform a split leap with circumduction

Figure-eight movements

a) <u>Figure-eights in the frontal plane.</u> Figure-eights are performed in front of and behind the body. Start with rope open at the front, one end in each hand. Arms remain parallel during the entire movement. Circle rope up left side to the vertical line, circle rope to the right behind the head and continue the movement from right to left in the back. When the rope descends again from the vertical, return to initial position at the front. Perform the movement in both directions.

When performing figure-eights, combine with:

√ Side lunge

√ One step, then hold a balance while swinging the rope over the head

It is possible to move the arms alternately in front of and behind the body during figure-eights. Start with rope open and one end on each hand, arms open and extended to the sides. Swing right arm up the right side to the vertical line and follow with left arm. Perform a circle behind the head with right arm. As the right arm descends in front of the body, the left arm performs a circle behind the head.

Having the arms out of phase as described provides an interesting alternation to the figure-eights. Change the direction of the figure-eights.

Perform the movement with:

√ Side body wave

√ Hold the rope at its center and perform the figure-eights as if the ends of the rope were clubs

b) <u>Figure-eights in the sagittal plane.</u> Hold rope open at the front, one end in each hand with arms parallel. Circle rope on the right side from the front to the rear. The rope circles up to the vertical and descends to circle on the left side, reaching the vertical from the rear. Start again. Change direction of the figure-eight.

This element can be combined with:

√ Chassé with movement of the rope

√ Large kicks to the rear as the rope swings upward, each leg alternately

√ Right split leaps with rope circle at right side and the same to the left

Another possible variation is alternating figure-eights in the sagittal plane, which is the same movement with the arms out of phase.

Beginning with the right arm to the right side, swing it to the back and up to the vertical line. At this time the left arm starts moving back on the right side and up to the vertical. The right arm lowers on the left side to swing back and up to the vertical, followed by the left hand. Change the direction of the figure-eight.

Combine the following movements:

√ Perform a body wave forward with figure-eights of the rope

√ Lift leg to the rear and hold a balance as the rope passes behind the body twice

√ Hold a balance with figure-eights, changing the position of the free leg

√ Hold rope at its center and perform figure-eights as if the ends of the rope were clubs

c) <u>Figure-eights in the horizontal plane above and below the head.</u> Hold the rope in front, one end in each hand with the arms parallel. Swing the rope horizontally from the right to the left, performing a complete circumduction with the rope and torso. Return to the starting position and complete a rope circle in front of the body. Start again. Execute the movement in both directions.

Combine with:

√ Turn on one foot during circle overhead and turn on heels (legs straight) during low circle

√ Large body circumduction during the circle overhead

√ Chassé during the circle overhead and jump over rope during the low circle

Alternating figure-eights can also be executed in the horizontal plane. Repeat the horizontal figure-eight with a phase shift similar to the figure-eights in the frontal and sagittal planes.

Start with a right arm swing from the right to the left, followed by the left arm. Move right arm from left to right behind the head, then from right to left in front to finish the low circle. Left arm follows movement of the right. Perform the movement in both directions.

Variations:

√ Combine with forward and backward bends of the torso

√ Combine with a body wave

√ Put in another circle with the rope in front of the body

√ The same as the previous figure-eights, hold the rope at its center

COMMON MISTAKES IN THE EXECUTION OF ROPE SWINGS AND CIRCLES AND METHODS OF CORRECTION

a) Alteration of the shape of the rope during the movement.

b) Imperfect movements, not considering the plane during the movement of the rope, and consequently touching the body with the rope.

Method of correction related to alteration of the shape of the rope during the movement

This is caused by a lack of coordination between the movement of the rope and the body. The rope must move with the same speed as the body, which is driving the movements of the rope. If one of the two moves faster or slower than the other one, the rope will lose its harmony with the body and thus lose its shape.

Exercises: Perform the following elements progressively, using both hands and all the planes:

√ Swings   √ Circles

√ Circumductions   √ Figure-eight movements

Examples: Very wide, slow swings in the frontal plane, combined with movement of the body. Also do these swings in the sagittal plane.

Circles first in the frontal plane to the right and left, then in the sagittal plane forward and backward, and finally in the horizontal plane in front of the body and overhead.

Circumductions, first in the frontal and sagittal planes, then in the horizontal plane. Perform these movements standing, kneeling and lying down.

Figure-eights. It is recommended to perform the arm movements first without the rope, and to introduce the rope later.

It is necessary to achieve sufficient coordination of the body and rope for the above-mentioned movements, since these will be combined to make elements.

The simplest figure-eight is in the sagittal plane to the right and left sides of the body. Next in difficulty is the figure-eight in the horizontal plane, overhead and in front, and finally in the frontal plane in front of and behind the body.

All ofthese exercises can be practiced in pairs. The partner checks the movement of the rope, warning the gymnast when the rope loses its shape. Correcting each other helps both girls to perform the movement, since each girl will remember the mistakes made by her partner and will try to avoid them.

Methods of Correction Related to Imperfect Movements

The movement of the arms must be as large as possible, keeping rope away from the body, making the movement larger and more continuous than with the arms flexed. If the rope moves out of plane during the movement, it is penalized for loss of shape and for touching the body.

Exercises: Perform the exercises of group a) following the same sequence. Perform them first with arms close to the body, flexed or bent, counting the number of repetitions before the rope stops, touches the body or loses its shape.

Perform the same exercise with arms extended away from the body, reaching their full length, until the rope stops or exceeds by five the same exercise done with arms close to the body. In this exercise the gymnast realizes the benefits of performing exercises to their full amplitude. The gymnast must achieve a higher number of correct repetitions with arms extended than with arms bent. If this does not happen, look for the cause of the problem (bad coordination between rope and body, excessive short length of the rope, etc.).

To help keep the plane, place gymnasts close to a wall or in pairs with both girls circling the rope in the same plane (one in front of the other for the frontal plane, side by side for the sagittal plane). If the ropes brush the wall or cross each other, one or both ropes must have lost the plane.

Game

Objective: To develop coordination with a partner, amplitude in the movement and concentration. The object of the game is to continuously perform elements with the rope, keeping in rhythm with the music.

Exercise: Divide the group into pairs. One of the two girls creates the movements and the other one imitates them. In order for the partner to imitate the movements, the leader must perform the movements with great amplitude. The girls trade tasks when a mistake is made. If the pair reaches the end of the

Follow the Leader with Rope

music without mistakes, they trade tasks when the music starts again. To make the game more difficult, trade tasks each time the coach indicates.

A mistake is when:

√ The rope stops

√ Coordination between the gymnasts is incorrect

√ Execution of the movements is incorrect

SMALL JUMPS

Small jumps through the rope can be performed:

√ With turns in the following directions:

- Forward

- Backward

- Sideward

√ At a certain speed:

- Slow — two jumps with one rope turn

- Normal — one jump with one rope turn

- Fast — one jump with two or three rope turns

√ With the rope:

- Open (each end on one hand)

- Crossing and uncrossing

While performing small jumps with the rope, the rhythm must be changed for different parts of the routine. If the tempo is slow, two small jumps or steps can be performed during one turn of the rope, which requires the arms to be extended. For a medium tempo, one jump fits in each turn, and for a fast rhythm two or three turns for one jump is appropriate. The arms must be straight but not tense, with the rope movement coming from the wrist.

It is very important for the gymnast to learn jumping technique in all three directions at all three speeds to show variety and difficulty in the elements. Great attention must be paid to the landings of the small jumps.

Small jumps can be:

   √ Jump from two feet, land on two feet

   √ Jump from two feet, land on one foot

   √ Jump from one foot, land on two feet

   √ Jump from one foot, land on the same foot

   √ Jump from one foot, land on the other foot

The small jumps are separated into two large groups, based on a kinetic point of view:

   a) Jumps/hops in place

   b) Jumps/hops with travel

Jumps/hops in place

a) <u>The boat.</u> With feet together and legs extended, swing rope front and back, jumping over the rope as it swings.

   Variations:

   √ Hop from one foot to the other

   √ Jump and cross the feet

   √ Jump with rhythmic traveling steps

b) <u>Jumps with rope turns.</u> Hold one end of the rope in each hand, arms extended to the sides. Swing the rope forward as the legs extend. Jump over the rope with turns forward and backward.

   Variations:

   √ Hop from one foot to the other, alternating

   √ Jump and cross the feet

   √ Jump and open legs to split, right to left

√ Jump and bend legs up to chest

√ Hop with one leg stretched, the other one bent

c) <u>Turns of the rope with change of directions.</u> Extend arms to sides. Hold one end of the rope in each hand and turn rope forward. Swing arms and rope overhead to the vertical and turn body 180° to the left. Arms lower behind the body and open to jump over the rope backward. Turn 180° to the left again when arms are vertical over the head. Repeat the element.

Variations:

√ Use all the variations from exercise b)

√ Combine a tuck jump and a jump with one or two legs extended

√ Combine a split jump and a jump with one leg stretched and the other one bent

d) <u>Jump forward crossing the arms.</u> Arms extended, rope behind body. Begin the rope turn with a swing upward. When the rope moves in front of the body, cross the arms as far as possible and jump over the forward rope turn. When the rope returns overhead, open arms and do a basic jump. Change the direction.

e) <u>Double jump and triple jump.</u> Arms extended, rope open. One end in each hand. Jump over a forward turn once to gain speed, then turn the rope twice during a single jump.

Variations:

√ Perform steps forward while jumping

√ Combine two basic jumps, one crossed, two basic, two crossed

When jumping backward, the arm cross is also done at head height. Uncross the arms as the rope is moving upward. This is more difficult than forward jumps with arm cross.

Variations:

√ Use all the variations from exercise "b"

√ Combine a double jump forward and a basic jump backward; repeat several times

√ Perform a double jump crossing the arms

√ Perform a double jump crossing arms on the first turn and opening on the second turn

√ Perform a series of four double jumps in a row, changing position of the arms and legs

The triple jump is done like the double jump, but turning the rope three times during one jump. This is of high difficulty.

Jumps/hops with travel

a) <u>Step-Leap, Step-Leap.</u> Turn rope forward with arms extended to the sides. Hold one end of the rope in each hand. When the rope is over head, step forward on the right leg then jump over forward turn onto the left leg. Start again from the right step. Change legs. Turn the rope backward and repeat.

Variations:

√ Perform a stag leap

√ First leap normal, second one long and low over the rope

b) <u>Chassé over the rope.</u> Hold rope open and perform a chassé to the right. Jump over the forward rope turn during the flight of the chassé with legs together. Reverse sides. Change the direction of the rope.

Variations:

√ Combine a chassé to each side, alternating

√ Chassé and cat leap over the rope

√ Chassé and jump through the rope with a cabriole

c) <u>Runs.</u> Hold rope open, one end in each hand. Perform two running steps during the rope turn, jumping over the rope on the third step.

Variations:

√ Turn 180° to the left after jumping over the rope forward. Take two steps backward during the rope turn and jump over the rope backward on the third step. Turn again left to repeat

√ Jump over the rope with small prances

√ Jump over the rope with a forward scissors

COMMON MISTAKES IN THE EXECUTION OF SMALL JUMPS/HOPS AND METHODS OF CORRECTION

a) Broken body.

b) Lack of dynamism.

Methods of Correction Related to a Broken Body

A broken body is one with the shoulders inclined forward, knees bent and feet not stretched. Small jumps must be done with the body straight, the shoulders pulled back slightly and the chin lifted. The feet and knees are extended during the flight and flexed on the landing.

Exercises:

1) Perform small jumps/hops varying only the position of the legs. Focus on one imaginary spot on the ceiling. This spot is the end of the prolongation of the arm as it is stretched diagonally upward to the ceiling.

   Hold arms in the simplest position, open to the sides, and turn rope from the wrist. In this position, the rope can be turned backward and forward, elevated or swung on the floor.

   Perform little jumps/hops:

   √ Two feet

   √ One foot, right or left

   √ Alternating right and left

   Combine the three previous exercises, for example: right foot, both feet, left foot, both feet. Right, left, both. Perform the same foot movements with rope turning backward.

2) Perform different arm movements with the rope.

   Circles (with both arms):

   √ In front of the body

   √ Behind the body

√ Over the head

√ Lateral (on the right side, on the left side)

Combine circles with jumps over the rope.

√ Cross the arms in front and behind the body

√ Combine the crosses with small jumps/hops, arms open or circling

√ Double jumps

√ Combine forward jump, cross jump, backward jump, double jump, etc.

Method of Correction Related to the Lack of Dynamism

The jumps must be quick and executed without support of the heel, except when continuing with another movement. High elevation is not required for jumps/hops. However, it is very imnportant to have a quick and agile take-off. The next jump/hop must start immediately after touching the floor from the previous jump.

Exercise:

On the floor draw a straight line, a curved line and a circle.

1) Without stepping on the line perform small jumps/hops, requiring the gymnast to move with the correct foot.

Jump on two feet from one side of the line to the other without stepping on it:

√ To the front and back

√ Right and left

Alternate right and left foot:

√ To the front and back

√ Right and left

One foot to one side of the line, the other foot to the other side:

√ To the front and back

√ Right and left

Alternate the three previous exercises.

Turn between the jumps.

Partner Routine

2) Perform the previous jumping exercises stepping on the lines, moving around the circle and inside the circle. Combine with arm movements.

Game

Objective: To improve originality, dynamism, coordination and group dynamics.

Exercise: Individually, in pairs or in groups, each gymnast has her own rope. Allow 10 minutes for the gymasts to prepare their own routine or series of jumps. The girls must agree on the sequence of the exercises if they are in pairs or groups.

The game consists of performing different small jumps/hops without stopping the rope and varying only the position of the legs. The object is to complete the highest number of variations with the jumps.

Variations:

√ Use different planes

√ Combine different arm movements

Gymnasts are rewarded for showing as many variations in their arm and leg movements as possible.

JUMPS/LEAPS

In order to perform leaps with the rope, it is necessary to have good, clean technique with the elements as presented in the floor exercise chapter. The difficulty is in coordinating the movement of the rope with the leaps.

The technique and the variations of the rope during the jumps are similar to those explained in the section on small jumps/hops.

The rope can turn in the following directions:

√ Forward

√ Backward

√ Laterally

During leaps the gymnast can:

√ Cross the arms

√ Uncross the arms

The rope can take the following shapes:

√ Open, held at each end or the center

√ Folded in two parts, held by one hand or two hands

√ Folded in three parts

√ Folded in four parts, held by both hands

The turning of the rope during the leaps can be done at different speeds:

√ Normal — one leap during one turn

√ Slow — two leaps during one turn

√ Fast — one leap with two or three turns

Due to the complexity of organizing jumps/leaps, and since there are many possible variations, we will choose the simplest method from the didactic point of view. We will group the leaps as a function of rope handling as follows:

√ Leaps with the rope open and one end in each hand

√ Leaps with the rope folded and both ends in one hand

Leaps with the rope open and one end in each hand

a) <u>Hold the rope behind the body with the arms extended to the sides.</u> Do two running steps. During the third step, jump in a tuck position over the forward turn of the rope and land on both feet.

Variations: Change the tuck jump to another type of leap:

√ Stag leap

√ Split jump

√ Scissors

Repeat the previous elements crossing the arms during the jump/leap.

b) <u>Rope open and arms extended to the sides.</u> Turning the rope forward, step forward with the right foot when the rope is overhead. Jump over the rope, bringing the legs together in the air (cabriole). Step again with the left foot and jump.

Variations:

√ Jump bringing the legs together in front of the body, above the horizontal

√ Perform the same jump closing the legs together behind the body. Turn the rope backward and step back on the right leg

√ Combine the jump with legs in front of the body (step forward left) and the jump with the legs behind the body (step right)

c) <u>Rope open with arms together at left side of body.</u> Make a circle forward on left side of body with a step on the left leg; circle forward on the right with a step on the right leg. Repeat step and circle to the left. When the arms are extended, separate the arms to open the rope and perform a split leap through the rope.

Variations: Instead of a split leap, perform the following:

√ Tuck jump

√ Side leap

√ Double stag leap

√ For higher difficulty turn the rope twice during the leap (double)

√ Combine two leaps (For example, a split leap followed by a tuck jump with three intermediary steps)

d) <u>Hold the rope open behind the body, arms extended to the sides.</u> Perform three running steps, turning the rope forward and stepping over the rope with each step. Perform a leap over the rope during fourth turn of the rope.

Step right, Step left, Step right, Leap

Variations:

√ Perform two or three split leaps in a row

√ Combine one split leap with a step and tuck jump

√ Same as above, turning the rope twice during the tuck jump

√ Combine split leap, step, side leap

e) <u>Rope open, arms extended and separated.</u> Perform a turning split leap passing through the rope.

Variations:

√ Perform a series of two turning leaps

√ Perform one normal turning leap followed by a turning leap to a ring position

f) <u>One end of the rope in each hand, hands together</u>. Circle the rope forward during a chassé. Perform a tuck jump with a half turn, jumping backward over the rope.

Variation:

√ Perform a double jump turning the rope backward

Leaps with the rope folded, both ends in one hand

a) <u>Hold both ends of the rope in the right hand.</u> Circle rope clockwise in the frontal plane during a chassé. Continue circles during the leap, exchanging rope to the left hand under the body.

Variations:

√ Perform a cat leap

√ Perform a split leap

√ Perform a stag leap

√ Perform a double stag leap

b) <u>Fold the rope in two parts, hold both ends in the right hand.</u> Perform two horizontal circles overhead. Jump over rope on the third horizontal circle underneath the legs.

Variations:

√ Perform a tuck jump

√ Perform a split leap

√ During the leap circle the rope over and under the body

√ Circle the rope twice under the body during one leap

c) <u>Hold rope with both ends in the right hand.</u> Perform a turning leap while circling rope overhead in the horizontal plane.

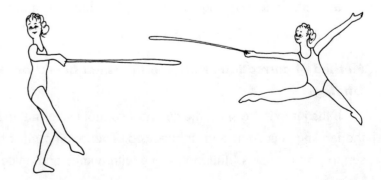

Variations:

√ Combine two turning leaps

√ Perform one turning leap, circling rope underneath body during the leap

√ Perform the same exercise, exchanging rope from hand to hand behind body during leap

√ Perform the same exercise, exchanging rope from one hand to the other under legs

d) Fold the rope in two, three or four parts (the more folds, the higher the difficulty). Hold the folded rope with one end in each hand. Jump forward over the folded rope. Jump backward.

Variations:

√ Jump over the rope twice in a row with knees bent

√ With rope folded in three parts, jump over with a stag leap

√ With rope folded in three parts, jump over with a split ring leap

√ Jump over rope with a split leap, land and perform a forward roll

COMMON MISTAKES IN THE EXECUTION OF JUMPS/LEAPS AND METHODS OF CORRECTION

a) Small height or length of the leaps and heavy landings.

b) Alteration in the shape of the rope.

Method of correction related to the small height or length and heavy landings

If the jump is too short the gymnast cannot perform the exercise correctly and the landing is sudden and unbalanced. The landing must be done with correct support on the sole of the foot, along with a knee and ankle bend to cushion the landing (*see* "Methods of correction for jumps" in Chapter 1).

Exercises: Perform leaps with the rope increasing the time of suspension in the air, height and le ngth of leaps, showing control at the time of landing.

Jumping exercises to improve the suspension

It is very important for the gymnast to land with her torso upright and the legs in demi-plié in order to spring from the landing into the next jump. Perform the exercises many times in a row spending as little time on the floor as possible. Avoid dropping the torso forward or bending the legs too deeply.

During the flight time:

√ Do small leaps in the air (increase the number of leaps in a row)

√ Perform small scissors

√ Extend and bend the legs, alternating

√ Double jumps with the rope with tuck jumps, straight jumps (varying the leg positions)

√ Cross and uncross the arms in front of the body, turning the rope in both directions

Jumps for height

Reach with the rope toward a certain height (a mark on the wall, a window or something similar, fasten a piece of paper onto a curtain, etc.):

√ With a push from the right leg, left leg or both simultaneously

√ While performing a tuck jump, scissors, double stag, etc.

Jumps for length

Leap past a mark on the floor, increasing the distance progressively:

√ With a split leap

√ With a side leap

Perform leaps which combine these three characteristics.

A single jump or double jump (as previously mentioned) with:

√ Cat leap

√ Leap from one step

√ Double stag leap from one step

Methods of correction to avoid alteration in the shape of the rope

Movement of the rope is too short and is irregular (different at each end or with vibrations). This is caused by a lack of amplitude of the movement in general, especially the arms, or by a lack of height, length and suspension during the leap. The body must remain in suspension long enough for the gymnast to move the arms in a wide motion. Proper arm movement allows for performance of the required elements with the legs.

Exercises:

1) Rope folded in two parts. One gymnast holds the folded rope with both ends in one hand. Her partner stands very close to her. The first gymnast circles the rope several times over the head and once under the body, with both gymnasts jumping over the rope. The gymnast circling the rope always performs a tuck jump. Her partner performs four jumps the same each time or each different. After finishing four jumps, the gymnasts transfer the rope from one to the other while circling overhead. Hold the rope first by the ends, then by the center with the rope doubled.

The difficulty of the exercise can be increased as follows:

√ Perform only one circle overhead and one circle under the body

√ Increase the speed of the rope circles

√ Transfer the rope to the partner circling overhead after each jump

√ Circle the rope twice under the body

2) With the rope open. Each gymnast holds one end of the rope. One gymnast turns the rope without jumping over it. Her partner is situated between the ends of the rope and performs jumps over the rope using the different exercises previously explained (with or without traveling). The gymnast who is not jumping over the rope must circle the rope as wide as possible. Her partner must move her arms in the same manner.

Game

Objective: To develop coordination between the rope and partners, amplitude in the movements and improvement in endurance with jumps.

Exercise: This game may also be played individually, each girl with her own rope. The reason for describing this game in pairs is to teach gymnasts to perform arm movements as wide as possible, requiring her partner to do the same. If one of the gymnasts shortens the movement, the rope will lose its shape and will either wrap around or touch the body.

Match pairs by height so that the rope has the same movement on both sides. Use ropes which are longer than normal or knot two ropes together and have the gymnasts wrap the ends around their hand. Each gymnast holds the end of the rope with her outer hand, keeping her inside shoulder close to her partner's.

The goal is to keep the movement of the rope continuous while jumping.

a) <u>Without traveling steps</u>. The gymnasts try to jump and surpass a certain height as many times as possible. Perform with tuck jumps, scissors, etc.

b) <u>With traveling steps</u>. Instead of working for increased vertical jump, as in the previous game, the gymnasts travel across the gym as far as possible, performing the least number of jumps. The gymnasts must then turn around when they reach the wall without stopping the rope. The gymnasts travel across the gym using small jumps/hops, circles overhead, etc. and return with a new travel in the opposite direction. Perfrom this exercise with small cat leaps, leaps, etc.

Each pair of gymnasts has three turns. Each time the rope stops is counted as one turn. The distance traveled after three turns is recorded. The goal is to reach the farthest distance with the least amount of jumps.

THROWS AND CATCHES

Throws and catches with the rope are very difficult. They must be performed with a smooth motion with the rope always moving so that the shape of the rope remains taut during the flight and the catch.

The throws can be executed with the rope as follows:

Extended	√ One hand
	√ Two hands
Open	√ One end in each hand
	√ Hands holding the center
Folded in two parts	√ One hand
	√ Two hands
Folded in three parts	√ One hand
	√ Two hands
Folded in four parts	√ One hands
	√ Two hands

During the flight the rope turns slow or fast, completing one, two or more rotations before it lands. The rope may not turn at all as is the case when the rope is thrown folded in three or four parts. The rotations may be in vertical, horizontal or oblique planes.

In preparation for throws the gymnast can use:

- Impetus
- Swings
- Circles
- Circumductions
- Figure-eight movements turns of the rope (with small jumps and leaps)

Different ways of catching the rope include:

At one end	√ One end in one hand
	√ One end in one hand, the other hand in the center
At both ends	√ Both ends in one hand
	√ One end in each hand
At the center	√ One hand
	√ Two hands together

After the rope is caught, the following movements can be performed:

   √ Swing — contrasting a quick movement with a slow movement

   √ Circles — without interrupting the movement of the rope

   √ Jumps — jump through the rope

   √ Wrapping — around any part of the body

   √ Balance movements — changing quickly from a fast movement to a static position

Release and catch of one end of the rope

a) <u>In the sagittal plane.</u> Hold one end of rope in the right hand with right arm behind the body. Free end of rope is extended behind the body. With a light pull and a demi-plié with the legs, swing right arm forward and upward to the diagonal, extending the legs. Free end returns to the left hand, held parallel to the right arm. Change to left hand. To vary the element catch free end with same hand as the pull.

Variations:

   √ Place rope extended in front of the body. Swing the rope backward to catch the free end with a slight arch of the back

   √ Catch the free end and continue into a front balance

   √ Perform a chassé with the rope pull and catch the end while jumping over the rope

b) <u>In the frontal plane.</u> Hold rope in the right hand extended toward left side of the body. Swing arm to the right and upward to the diagonal. Catch free end with the left hand. To vary the element catch rope with same hand as the pull.

Variations:

√ Perform a side body wave during the pull

√ Hold a balance until the free end is caught

√ Perform a side chassé with the rope pull. Catch the free end behind the body and perform a tuck jump with a ¹/₄ turn left after exchanging the free end of the rope to the other hand (right to left)

c) <u>In the horizontal plane.</u> Hold rope open, one end in each hand. Left arm remains stationary throughout the movement, extended vertically upward. Right arm is extended forward. Swing rope around to the right with the left wrist. Bend knees slightly and release rope when the right hand reaches as far to the left as possible. Extend knees and catch rope with the right when it returns to the starting position.

Perform the same exercise in the opposite direction, changing the positions of the arms.

Variations:

√ Perform the previous exercise releasing one end during a jump

√ Perform this exercise with a hand exchange. The right hand, which released the rope, exchanges with the left hand during the release. Arms change positions so that the left hand catches free end

d) <u>Throws with the rope extended.</u> Stretch rope behind the body, holding one end of the rope in the right hand. With a strong impulse swing arm forward to the vertical and release rope. Catch free end first, causing the end that was released to move close to the body. Catch this end with the other hand. Change hands.

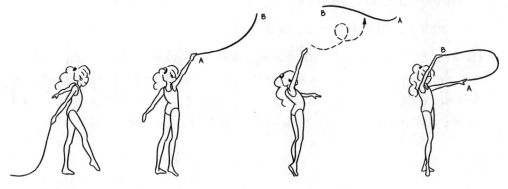

Variations:

√ Hold a balance during the flight of the rope

√ Throw the rope while doing a leap. Catch both ends, the first one during a chassé and the second one during a tuck jump while jumping over the rope (one end in each hand)

Throw and catch of the rope

a) <u>Rope with ends apart, one end in each hand.</u> Arms parallel. Swing rope in the frontal plane, in front of the body from right to left, and perform a small throw. Rope rotates clockwise in the air, passing over the head, to catch on the right side. Repeat in the opposite direction.

Variations:

√ Throw the rope. Lower to the floor in a side lunge, perform a side roll. Stand up to catch the rope and continue with circles

√ Throw the rope, perform an illusion turn. Catch the rope and continue with a swing

√ Repeat the two previous elements with a higher throw and with more rotations of the rope during the flight

√ Perform the previous elements holding rope with only one hand

b) <u>Hold rope with ends apart, one in each hand, arms extended to the right side of the body.</u> Swing rope backwards in sagittal plane. Perform a short, low throw forward with one rotation of the rope. Catch rope and continue with sagittal swings. Perform exercise to the left side. Throw rope to the back.

Variations:

√ Throw and catch during a double stag jump

√ Throw, roll forward and catch while holding a balance position

√ Throw to a greater height with rope completing several turns

√ Perform the previous elements holding rope with only one hand

c) <u>Total throw. One end in each hand.</u> Turn rope backward, jumping over it twice. Throw rope upward after the third jump. When the throw is performed without travel, rope is released directly over the head. When the throw is performed with travel steps, rope is released diagonally forward. Catch rope and continue with small jumps through the rope. Turn the rope forward to throw and catch.

Variations:

√ Catch the rope in place and combine with different types of little jumps, crossing and uncrossing the arms

√ Throw the rope with travel steps and catch with a big jump/leap over the rope. Tuck jump, double stag leap, etc.

√ Throw the rope with a double jump

√ Catch the rope with a double turn during a tuck jump

d) Total throw. Rope held at its center. Swing ends of the rope forward and backward. Throw rope in front of the body and catch it at the ends. Throw to the back.

Variations:

√ Throw, from circling the rope, to a greater height with the rope rotating several times while in the air. Perform a roll and catch the ends of the rope

√ Throw rope forward. Perform a leap to a forward roll. Catch the rope in a kneeling position

e) Fold the rope into three or four parts. Hold folded rope at both ends. Throw it over the head and catch each knotted end when the rope comes down.

Variations:

√ Throw rope during a split leap. Catch and continue with circles in a balance

√ Hold folded rope at one end and perform a high throw. Execute a 360° turn and catch the ends of the rope with a swing, making the movement smooth

COMMON MISTAKES IN THE EXECUTION OF THROWS AND CATCHES AND METHODS OF CORRECTION

a) Arm is flexed or bent at point of release of rope, causing an alteration in shape of rope.

b) Incorrect positioning of arm during throws with traveling steps.

c) Free end touches body or floor during the release and catch of one end of the rope.

Methods of correction related to the bending of the arm at the point of release

Throw must be done with arm at its maximum extension, close to the ear for jumping movements into the vertical throws and at varying positions for the other types.

Perform the follow exercises with focus on a correct throw and paying little attention to the catch: Who can throw rope to a certain height and catch without letting it touch the floor?

Increase the difficulty of the throws:

√ With a swing, circle, circumduction, jump, etc. before the throw

√ Throw the rope from different positions: on the knees, sitting, etc.

√ Lengthen or change the shape of the rope

Vary the throws:

√ With one or more rotations

√ Using different planes

√ With the rope extended or folded in two or four parts

Method of correction related to incorrect positioning of the arm during the throws with travel steps

The arm must be pointed diagonally in the direction of the travel.

Exercises:

Divide the gymnasts in pairs. One gymnast remains in one place with a rope. Her partner moves around her, stopping at a different spot each time.

Without changing her body position or moving her feet, the gymnast with the rope must throw the rope with arm extended and inclined toward her partner, wherever she is. The other gymnast catches the rope and throws it back to her partner from whatever position she has caught it (in front, to the side or backwards).

Every six or eight correct throws, the gymnast who was moving stays in place and vice versa.

It is important to insist that the gymnast moving around changes position enough to require the throws to be in all different directions and varying distances. The rope must also pass a certain height during the throw. Increase difficulty of the throws by adding small jumps with the rope before the throw, circles into the throw, and throws with the rope folded in two, four or more parts.

Methods of correction related to the touching of the free end on the floor or body during the one-end releases

Hold one end in one hand. The other end moves in different patterns and is caught to continue with other movements. The free end should not touch the floor or any part of the body. This will cause an alteration in the shape of the rope.

Exercises:

Release one end of the rope. Other hand holds other end and keeps the rest of the rope moving and making different figures (circles, swings, spirals, etc.). Continue until rope touches anything or shape is incorrect. Change hands.

Perform the previous exercise with different travels, little jumps, etc.

When the movement of the rope is controlled with one end free, perform a release of both ends and catch. Start first in a static position and then combine with travel steps and other elements, maintaining a progression based on the difficulty of elements.

COMMON MISTAKES AND METHODS OF CORRECTION IN THE CATCHING OF THE ROPE

a) Not catching the rope at the ends or at the center, whether extended or folded.

b) Catching the rope with an interruption of the motion.

These two mistakes must be corrected simultaneously because the second is a consequence of the first.

Methods of correction related to not catching rope at its ends or center, whether extended or folded

The rope must be caught at the center or by the ends. Any other way of catching is incorrect and increases the difficulty of continuing with an exercise.

Methods of correction to catch the rope without interrupting the motion

To achieve a continuous movement of the rope, it must be caught as far as possible from the body and followed by an element which moves in the same direction.

Exercises:

Perform the exercise from the previous section related to the correction of throws, paying special attention to catching the rope without stopping motion or catching in a static position as at the end of a routine. Perform the throws first with the gymnasts facing each other, without traveling. If the catch is done correctly, the gymnast continues performing elements with the rope in preparation for the next throw. If the catch is done incorrectly and the rope is not caught at the center or by the ends, the gymnast must stop the movement and let the end of the rope fall to the ground.

After practicing catches with rope in all directions and each gymnast is able to throw and catch correctly, progressively increase difficulty of throws and catches as mentioned previously.

Game

Objective: To control height of throw and catch correctly with the torso and arm extended.

Who is able to catch the rope after:

√ Touch the floor, sit down, lie down, etc.?

√ Crawl under the vault, between the partner's legs, etc.?

√ Jump onto stacked mats or something similar?

Rope Throw Game

√ Touch a spot in the gym and return to catch the rope?

√ Roll forward or backward on the floor?

Continue the movement of the rope with another movement.

The gymnast throws the rope after being given a signal. The ropes are thrown all at the same time or in groups, depending on the number of gymnasts. In order to perform the exercise correctly, the ropes must be thrown to a certain height.

Each girl tries to catch her rope first, which forces her to extend her arms and torso. The goal is to catch the rope as early as possible with the correct toss and catch technique.

WRAPPING AND BALANCES

Other movements that are performed with the rope are the wraps around the body. These movements provide variety to the routine.

Wrapping with the rope folded

a) <u>Wrap the rope folded in two parts.</u> Hold rope with two ends together in the right hand. Swing rope from left to right in preparation. Swing rope horizontal to the left to wrap rope around the waist. Hold right arm still. To unwrap rope pull with the right arm then continue swing to the right. Change hands.

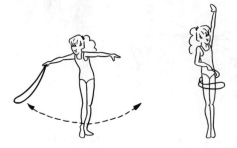

b) <u>Wraps around the arms.</u> Hold rope open, one end in each hand, arms extended to right side of the body. Perform forward rope turns with arms stationary to wrap rope around right arm. To unwrap turn rope in the opposite direction until it is free. Swing rope two times in preparation to start the wrapping. Perform wrap to the left. Do wrap turning the rope in both directions.

Variation:

√ Perform 180° turn to the left before unwrapping the rope

Wrapping with the rope extended

a) <u>Hold the rope open, one end in each hand</u>. Right arm is stretched to the vertical, left arm at waist height. Swing rope horizontal to the left and back. Hold the left arm still to wrap the rope around the body. To unwrap turn rope in the opposite direction.

Variations:

√ Wrap rope in both directions, changing positions of the arms

√ Turn body in opposite direction at same time that the rope is wrapping or unwrapping

√ Wrap and unwrap the rope during a waltz step

√ Wrap rope during a forward body wave, unwrap during a back body wave

b) <u>Wrapping with the rope fully extended.</u> Fold rope in two parts and hold in the right hand. Prepare with a swing to the right. Swing rope to the left, releasing one end to extend rope to its full length. Hold right arm still and turn body to the right (opposite direction of the rope) to wrap rope around body. Catch the free end when wrap is completed. Change hands and repeat to the other direction. This movement can be used as the end of a routine.

Variations:

√ Perform a turn element at same time as rope is wrapping and in the opposite direction.

√ Perform the same wrap around legs or feet while holding a balance or doing a turn.

Balance movements

The characteristics of rope allow for different types of skills that, like wrapping, are not recognized by the FIG Code of Points as a group of elements, but which provide variety in the composition.

Because of the length and flexibility of the rope, it is possible to perform balance exercises with the body, uniting any part of it with the apparus. The possibilities for these elements are unlimited, considering all the different positions of the legs, arms, trunk and head.

The different balance movements provide originality to the composition and give the gymnast a break from using the strength and speed necessary to move the rope. Balances can also be used as a beginning or ending to a routine.

a) <u>Holding the rope with two hands.</u> *Rope attached to the leg.* Hold one end of the rope in each hand and hook the center of the rope to the leg.

Variations:

√ With arms extended forward, lift right leg in front of body above the horizontal. Change legs

√ Perform the same exercise with leg to the side

√ With an arch of the back, lift right or left leg in front of the body past the horizontal. Extend arms to continue the line of the torso

√ With arms open and extended upward, perform a support on left knee and lift right leg in front of the body, holding rope on the foot

Stand on right leg with rope under right foot. Lift left leg bent in front of body with arms extended forward.

Same as the previous exercise with left leg extended behind the body.

Balance in arabesque with arms stretched upward. Hold one end of the rope in each hand and hook center on foot. Bring arms down in front of the body, lifting back leg up to a vertical line.

b) <u>Holding the rope in one hand.</u>

Variations:

√   Stand on one leg with the other extended in front of the body. Hold center of rope with foot and both ends in one hand

√   Same as the previous exercise lifting the leg to the side

√   Lift leg behind the body

c) <u>Balance with the rope folded in four parts, held with two hands.</u> The positions of the body and legs have unlimited variations.

√   Back arch

√   Side lunge

√   Side bend static position

COMMON MISTAKES IN THE EXECUTION AND METHODS OF CORRECTION

a) Incomplete wrapping.

b) Rough wrapping.

c) Balance errors.

Method of correction related to incomplete wrapping

The rope does not wrap completely if the gymnast bends her arm, giving too little impulse for the wrap, or if she separates her arms excessively when starting the wrap. The wrap will be incomplete if the unwrap starts too early, not allowing the rope to finish the inital wrapping.

Exercises:

Perform wraps with the rope around different objects in the gym (column, stairs, bars, etc.). The gymnast moves as close as possible to the object with the arms extended. With a strong impulse the gymnast wraps her rope around the object and waits for the free end to touch the surface before starting the unwrapping.

By performing this exercise on a visible surface, the gymnast can see the movement of the rope more clearly. Perform the exercises using both hands and changing positions — front, side, backward; high, middle or low on the object.

Method of correction related to a rough wrap

When wrapping the rope at a high speed with excessive impulse, the length of the rope changes very quickly. The rope then hits the gymnast at the end of the movement.

Exercises:

In pairs, perform wraps on the partner first around the waist, which is the least sensitive part of the body, then move to the legs, feet and arms. If the rope is used like a whip, the gymnast who is receiving the rope could be hurt. The object of this exercise must be understood and explained with great care.

When the smoothness of the wrapping is achieved practice the wraps individually around the neck, which is the most sensitive part of the body.

Method of correction related to balance errors

Balance errors with rope are the same as those in Chapter 1. Many times the rope helps the gymnast maintain balance, but does not help to completely control it. The ability to maintain balance correctly must be achieved by practicing balances without apparatus, and then adding the rope, which links two parts of the body.

Game

Objective. To improve originality, attention and dynamism in the performance of a wrap.

Exercise. The object of the game is to perform as many wraps around the body as possible. During each wrap the gymnasts must hold their balance on the toes on one or two feet. Example: wrapping the rope around the waist while balancing on one foot.

The exercises are done individually and in rhythm with the music. Each gymnast has a partner who counts the number of wraps. A gymnast is not allowed to repeat two wraps on the same part of the body, even if done in opposite directions. The balances may be repeated. The goal is to reach the highest number of wraps without stopping the rope.

Variation:

√   Try it in pairs

MUSICAL ACCOMPANIMENT

The rope requires strong, lively music with accents for the throws and rapid rhythms for the jumps and hops. Since the rope is not very showy, the music must have marked contrasts to make the routine with the apparatus interesting.

The music used should not be the same throughout. Use compositions having sections with 2/4 meter, incorporating slow parts in order to show maximum amplitude.

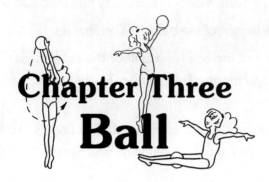

Chapter Three
Ball

This apparatus was incorporated into the World Championships in 1969, in Varna, Bulgaria, but it has been in existence since ancient times.

Balls were used in children's games and as apparatus in many sports, before being introduced into rhythmic gymnastics. It is one of the favorite apparatus for young girls and now it is considered the "hottest" apparatus in competitions.

Handling the ball is possible with a little knowledge of the technique. The gymnast can become familiar with the ball at an early age. By developing the proper technique, she will be able to treat the ball as a part of her body, thereby embellishing and elongating each movement.

CHARACTERISTICS AND FUNDAMENTALS OF THE APPARATUS

The ball can be made of rubber or synthetic material (flexible plastic) as long as it has the same elasticity as rubber.

The official diameter, set by the FIG, is 18-20 cm. For small girls who are just beginning, a 14-17 cm diameter ball can be used.

When it is necessary to have a large number of balls on hand, it is beneficial to have balls of different diameters, which forces the gymnast to develop good habits.

All colors are allowed. Several colors may be combined on one ball.

The minimum weight of the ball is 400 grams.

The movement of the ball is a result of the movement of the body and both must be perfectly synchronized with music. The ball should never be held in a static position.

The ball should rest in the palm hand. The fingers are together and flexed, following the shape of the ball. The fingers never grasp the ball, they only support the weight.

Different methods of holding the ball

TWO HANDS

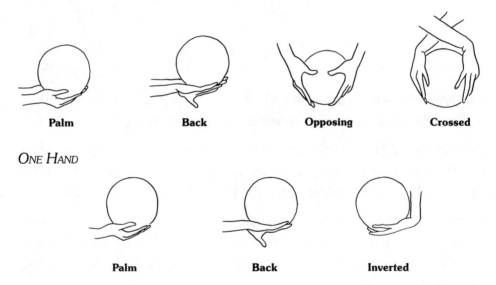

| Palm | Back | Opposing | Crossed |

ONE HAND

| Palm | Back | Inverted |

The ball, because of its shape and the material it is made of, has possibilities for a great variety of elements. Fundamental elements include bounces, a group of elements possible only with the ball, rolls on the floor and over the body, and throws and catches. Other elements are the rotations, balances of the ball on the hand, and swings and circles which are common to all the apparatus. The movements can be executed in all planes and directions, with one or both hands or continually transferring the ball from one hand to the other.

The ball, a compact and relatively small apparatus, presents no special difficulty in the use of different planes or shifting from one to another. It requires movement of large amplitude, achieving (with exceptions) the largest possible radius the body or arm and ball can draw, since the movement of the ball is a consequence of the total movement of the body.

BASIC TECHNIQUE

The group of elements of the basic technique for this apparatus are:

√ Circular motions (swings, circumductions and figure-eights)

√ Bounces

√ Rotations

√ Rolls

√ Throws

√ Movements with the ball balanced on the hand

The first group of elements, common to all the apparatus, deals with momentum, *swings and circumductions*. For the execution of these elements, the ball must rest on the hand, neither gripped nor pressed against the wrist. The amplitude of these movements is fundamental, since the further away the ball is from the body, the wider the movement that is achieved with the body. Ball elements can be combined with almost all of the body elements from the free exercise.

Bounces are the most familiar elements to the gymnast, because many of the games played by children include bouncing a ball. When bouncing, the descending movement of the ball must be accompanied by bending the legs. The legs extend as the ball rises, so the body movement is coordinated with the bounce. It is important to push the ball towards the floor, not to hit it, keeping the hand in the shape of the ball. Independent of the body position, the hand follows the ascending movement of the ball in order to make a quiet, controlled catch.

There is not a great variety of *rotations* with the ball. This is because while the ball rotates, it can not travel. It must remain on the floor or a part of the body: chest, knees, hand, fingers. Therefore, the variety of elements is limited. It is possible, however, to create variety by coordinating the rotations with different body elements of the free exercise. For the rotations, the hand must be adapted (as in all the movements with this apparatus) to the shape of the ball as it turns on its vertical axis, in both directions.

Rolls, a group of elements which presents more variety, are most characteristic of this apparatus. For rolls on the floor, the arm is extended to initiate the movement. The ball is moved smoothly through the maximum extension of the arm and out to the fingertips. The ball must not bounce during the roll on the floor. To catch the ball, the movement is reversed. Start at the fingertips and roll the ball up to the palm of the hand. The ball can also be caught with the feet.

When rolling the ball over the body, it must roll smoothly without interruption or bouncing over any part of the body. Rolls are performed in all directions by varying the position of the body.

When the rolling surface is parallel to the floor, the roll can be initiated by pushing with the free hand or by elevating that part of the body, inclining the surface to facilitate the roll.

At the end of the roll, the ball can be stopped by using the free hand or by elevating that part of the body which serves as the rolling surface, decreasing the speed of the ball. The ball then comes to rest on the palm of the hand or another part of the body.

Throws with the ball can be performed with one or two hands and sometimes with the feet, presenting many variations. The impulse for the throw starts with a slight bend and extension of the legs. The extension continues along the body, arm, and out to the fingertips. The body and arm stretch in the direction of the throw. To catch the ball, the movement is the same but in reverse. The gymnast waits for the ball to descend with the body and arm stretched. Catching the ball, with one or two hands, involves the whole body. The ball rolls from the fingertips into the palm of the hand. The arm, body and legs continue the downward movement of the ball, absorbing its weight and making the catch smooth and noiseless.

In movements with the ball *balanced on the hand*, the ball rests on the palm or the back of the hand during inside and outside rotation movements with the arm, or with changes of body position.

For the ball to be balanced on the back of the hand, the hand must be situated parallel to the floor without tension or rigidity, allowing it to adapt to the shape of the ball. For the ball to balance on the palm of the hand, the hand must be relaxed, adapting the shape of the ball. The ball must avoid contact with the wrist or the forearm, which could cause the ball to drop off the hand.

Great amplitude is imperative in the execution of these ball elements in order to achieve continuity and smoothness which are fundamental characteristics in the handling of the ball.

CIRCULAR MOTIONS

Swings, Circumductions and Figure Eights

The avoidance of grasping the ball is especially important during the execution of circular motions. To avoid grasping the ball, it is important to achieve perfect coordination between the movements of the body and those of the ball.

During the performance of these elements, the ball is always in contact with the hands. If contact is lost it becomes another type of element.

Swings, circumductions and spirals can be done as follows, always accompanied by movement with the free arm:

With one hand or both hands:

√ Normal positions of the arm or internal rotation of the arms

In the planes:

√ Frontal in front or in back

√ Sagittal front to back or back to front

√ Horizontal above the head or below head level

The free hand can move together with the movement of the ball either alternating, parallel or in opposition.

Swings

a) <u>Swings in the frontal plane.</u>

   1) Swing the ball, held in both hands, from right to left and vice versa. Accompany the swing with a flexion and extension of the legs.

Variations:

√ Swing, standing with legs apart, shifting weight toward side where ball is pointed

√ With a cross step to the side, swing to both sides

√ Repeat the previous elements, swinging ball behind the body

2) Swing the ball, held in one hand, to the right and left, combined with a flexion and extension of the legs. Use both hands.

Variations:

√ Perform side lunge while swinging ball to the side

√ Combine with a side body wave

√ Step and arabesque hop on the right leg while swinging ball to the right. Repeat to left

√ Combine with small running steps

3) Swing the ball, exchanging the ball from hand to hand in front of the body. Perform this exercise along with a flexion and extension of the knees.

Variations:

√ Exchange the ball from hand to hand during a waltz step

√ On one knee with the other leg extended in front of the body, exchange the ball from hand to hand under the extended leg

√ Chassé and perform a tuck jump, exchanging the ball from hand to hand over the head

√ Chassé, perform a tuck jump, exchanging the ball from hand to hand under the body

4) Swing ball in the right hand to the right with an inward rotation of the arm, and to left with an outward rotation of the arm. Palm of the hand faces upward during both swings. Perform this exercise with a flexion and extension of the legs. Use the other hand.

Variations:

√ Waltz step to the right and to the left

√ Step forward with the right leg, lifting the other leg to the back, with the swing to the right. Step with the left leg when swinging to the left side

b) <u>Swings in the sagittal plane.</u>

1) Swing the ball, held with two hands, to front and back on both sides of the body. Accompany swing with a flexion and extension of the legs.

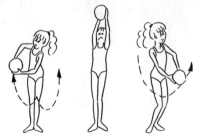

Variations:

√ Bend the torso forward as the ball swings backward. Lift the torso with the swing forward

√ Step forward and close the legs together with the forward swing; step backwards and close the legs together during the backwards swing

2) Swing ball, held in one hand, from the back to the front and vice versa. Perform this along with a flexion and extension of the legs. Use both hands alternately.

Variations:

√ Coordinate with forward lunge when the ball is moving backwards, and backward lunge when the ball is moving forward

√ Coordinate with running steps backward and forward

√ Kneeling, swing ball a few times and perform a toe rise during swing from front to back

3) Swing ball and exchange from hand to hand in front and behind body. Coordinate this exercise with a flexion and extension of the legs.

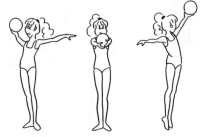

Variations:

√ Swing ball forward and exchange with a backward leg kick, bending the support leg

√ Swing ball backwards, transferring it from hand to hand during a front balance

4) Swing ball, held with one hand, with an inward rotation of the arm. Swing ball forward and rotate the arm inward to swing the ball backward. Coordinate this exercise with a flexion and extension of the legs. Alternate hands.

Variations:

√ Coordinate with a waltz step forward

√ Step forward and extend the legs and body upward, arms extended to the vertical. Do a second step rotating the arms inward and bending the body forward and bending the legs. Contrast the stretching movement with the contraction

√ Chassé forward during the forward swing and perform an arabesque hop during the backward swing

c) Swings in the horizontal plane.

1) Swing ball from the right to the left and vice versa. Hold with both hands. Sit in a kneeling position.

Variations:

√ Sit to the right side of the feet when swinging to the left, and sit to the left side of the feet when swinging to the right

√ Standing, flex and extend the legs while swinging to the right and left. Extend legs when ball is pointed to the right and the left side, and bend as the ball passes in front of the body

2) Swing ball from the left to the right, held in one hand. Legs apart, shift the weight from one leg to the other. Alternate hands.

Variations:

√ Maintain balance on two feet on the toes, swinging ball at shoulder height, with as much elongation of the body as possible

√ Coordinate with a waltz step forward

√ Coordinate with side body wave to the right and left, coinciding with the swing

3) Swing the ball right and left, exchanging it from hand to hand in front of the body. Coordinate with a shifting of the weight with the legs apart.

Variations:

√ Coordinate with a circle step (see Chapter 1), exchanging ball in front of the body

√ Step forward with one leg and exchange the ball from hand to hand while holding a balance in arabesque. The support leg is extended with the other leg held at horizontal behind the body, coordinated with the swing

CIRCUMDUCTIONS

a) Circumductions in the frontal plane.

1) Circumductions with ball held with both hands. Walk forward with a circumduction to the right, incline the torso toward the ball. Change direction.

Variations:

√ Perform sides lunges to both sides, coordinating with the circumduction

√ Side chassé to the right and step to an arabesque hop during the swing. Repeat to the left

√ Turn on two feet while doing a circumduction with the ball (spiral turn)

2) Circumduction with ball held with one hand, exchanging it to the other hand overhead or at the bottom of the circle. Change direction.

Variations:

√ Lunge on the back leg, exchanging the ball overhead. Step forward to kick the leg backwards, exchanging the ball again overhead

√ Perform a 360° turn during the circumduction. Turn 180° left exchanging the ball from the right hand to the left over the head. Continue the turn 180°

√ Chassé forward exchanging the ball overhead. Perform a cat leap, exchanging the ball under the legs

√ Do the previous exercise with a split leap forward

b) Circumductions in the sagittal plane.

1) Circumductions holding the ball with both hands, forward and backward, to both sides of the body and in both directions. Hold the balance on the toes.

Variations:

√ Kneeling, perform circumduction to the right and left sitting to the opposite side of the circles

√ Coordinate with a forward waltz step with turn. Swing ball up during steps forward and lower during steps backward

2) Circumduction to both sides of the body, ball held with one hand. Exchange ball from hand to hand in front of the body. Do little steps during the circumduction. Change direction.

Variations:

√ Hold a balance on one leg during the circumduction

√ Do running steps and slide down onto the floor. Start the forward circumduction with a chassé and finish as the body lowers to the floor

c) <u>Circumductions in the horizontal plane.</u>

1) Circumduction holding the ball with both hands. Perform circles in both directions. Coordinate with a body circumduction.

Variations:

√ Do circumduction with a deep arch of the back. Weight remains on the back leg with front leg extended

√ Do circumduction in a kneeling position on the floor

2) Circumduction holding ball with one hand. Coordinate movement of the torso and free arm. Use both arms and both directions.

Variations:

√ In a seated position, do a side scale turning onto the hip. The arm moves horizontally without touching the floor

√ On one knee with the other leg extended forward. With lateral support on o
   one arm, do circumduction along with flexion of the torso. When ball is
   behind body, lift the supporting knee. Lower knee when the ball moves
   forward

√ Exchange ball from hand to hand, in front or behind the body

COMMON MISTAKES IN THE EXECUTION OF CIRCUMDUCTIONS AND METHODS OF CORRECTION

a) holding ball against the forearm

b) incorrect handling of the ball

Methods of correction

The correction of these two mistakes can be achieved simultaneously with some methods, so they will be examined together. The common characteristic is that the ball does not freely rest in the palm of the hand, either because it is gripped with the fingers or because the forearm is helping to hold the ball on the hand.

The palm of the hand must match the shape of the ball at all times. This is achieved by keeping the wrist and fingers slightly relaxed and without resting the ball against the forearm.

It is highly recommended during practice, to teach the gymnast that it is better to let the ball fall on the floor than to acquire the habit of bending the wrist, causing the ball to be held against the forearm.

Exercises:

Lift the weight of the ball toward the fingertips, hold it there a few seconds and return it to the palm of the hand.

Roll ball from the palm of the hand to the fingers:

√ On one hand   √ On the other hand

√ On both hands together

Perform swings in the frontal, sagittal, and horizontal planes:

√ With ball on one hand   √ With ball on the other hand

√ Exchanging ball from hand to hand *every* four swings

√ Same as the previous exercise, but *every* two swings

Add musical accompaniment in the next exercises, using different rhythms (fast and slow) so the gymnasts learn to adapt rhythms to the movement of the ball.

Combine swings and circumductions in each plane:

√ One swing, one circumduction   √ Two swings, two circumductions

√ One swing, three circumductions

Perform the swings and circumductions in the frontal, sagittal and horizontal planes in both directions.

Game

Objective: To develop coordination with music and a partner while holding the ball.

Exercise: Each pair has one ball. The location of each gymnast (facing each other, to the side or behind the partner) depends on the plane in which the ball is moving.

One gymnast holds the ball and performs two swings and two circumductions in the same plane. After two more swings, the gymnast passes the ball to her partner who performs the same exercise in the same plane.

Partner Swing Game

The object of the game is to keep the ball moving, held correctly, as long as possible without dropping on the floor.

For beginners, the exercise is accompanied by music or percussion with a slow rhythm. For advanced gymnasts, alternate slow and fast rhythms continuously changing the movement of the ball.

Proceed as follows to change from one plane to another: One gymnast performs two swings and two circumductions. After two more swings in the same plane, she passes the ball to her partner who changes the plane. The partner must be correctly located to receive the ball and perform the entire exercise in the new plane and so on.

The game is over when the ball is dropped or the handling of the ball is incorrect.

For higher level gymnasts, the game ends when not all planes and directions have been used before repeating the same one more than twice or there is an absence of harmony between music and movement.

The goal is to continue performing the exercises as long as possible without mistakes.

BOUNCES

Bounces are the characteristic movements of the ball and are extraordinarily interesting from the rhythmic standpoint.

Bounce the ball by pushing it, not by hitting it. This amount of acceleration is enough for the ball to bounce to a sufficient height. When pushing the ball for a bounce, the hand must follow the movement and direction of the bounce.

To catch the ball, the hand must adapt itself to the shape of the ball during the ascending movement, finishing with the ball on the palm or back of the hand. Catching the ball with the feet is also possible. In both cases, catches must be done without noise.

To perform a series of bounces or to initiate a bounce, it is necessary to coordinate the exercise with flexion and extension of the ankles, knees and hips.

Start the bounce holding the ball away from the body at arm's length to control direction and intensity of the bounce.

Repeated bouncing of the ball with no contact with a part of the body is considered a fault.

The bounce can be done:

√ With vertical trajectory √ With an oblique trajectory of 45°

Bounces may be done:

√ On the floor — in front, side, back, in a circle

√ On the body

Bounces on the floor may be pushed by:

√ One or two hands √ Palm or back of hand

√ Chest √ Elbow

√ Knee √ Foot

Bounces on the body may be done with the:

√ Shoulder √ Chest

√ Knee √ Foot

√ Back

Ball can be caught with:

√ One hand or both hands √ Palm or back of hands

√ Feet

Bounces can be done in place without traveling or with small steps, running steps, traveling leaps, etc.

Bounces on the floor

a) *Bouncing the ball with both hands.*

1) Drop ball in front of body, holding with both hands. Hands together, palms facing upward, let ball drop to the floor and catch after a swing of the arms.

Variations:

√ Drop ball, bend knees to a squat position and catch with backs of both hands

√ Drop ball at right side of body, arms extended vertically over head. Catch ball with right hand on same side of body with a side bend of the torso

√ Let ball drop behind the body, turn 180° and catch with one hand, one knee bent, the other in front of the body

2) Bounce ball in front of body. Coordinate with a flexion and extension of the knees. Bounce ball several times in a row.

Variations:

√ During four consecutive bounces, slowly lower body to a squat position by bending the legs. Return to standing with another four consecutive bounces

√ Bounce ball in front of body and do a forward arm circumduction. Finish circle with arms at vertical, holding balance on the toes. Ball must reach the level of the hands

√ Mark rhythms with:

• 2 high bounces, 2 low bounces

• 1 high bounce, 3 low bounces

• 3 high bounces, 1 low bounce, etc.

√ Hold ball with arms crossed, bounce and catch again with arms crossed

b) Bouncing the ball with one hand.

1) Bounce ball with palm or back of hand in front of body. Catch ball with two hands, on palms or backs of the hands. Coordinate with flexion and extension of the legs. Use both hands.

Variations:

√ Swing arms smoothly during the bouncing

√ Bounce ball, turn 90° to catch in a side bend. Legs together and extended

√ Bounce ball at side of body on one single point. Walk in a circle around the ball

√ Bounce ball, perform a turn on one leg and catch ball in front of body

2) Bounce ball alternating hands. Bounce ball at right side of body with right hand. Turn 90° to the right and bounce with left hand. Perform this exercise with arm swings.

Variation:

√ Bounce the ball three times in the same spot. On the fourth bounce turn 360° and catch with one hand

3) Bounce ball around body without moving. Use both hands and bounce around in both directions. Bounce ball to the right turning torso to the right. Bounce behind the body and quickly turn to the left to continue bouncing at left side and then to front with right hand. Coordinate with flexion and extension of the legs. Change directions.

Variations:

√ Bounce ball to the right, changing hands when turning body to the left. Bounce with left hand at the first possible moment

√ Bounce ball around the body, alternating hands for each bounce

√ Repeat previous elements bouncing ball while sitting with legs bent and together

4) Bounce ball in an oblique trajectory in front of body, exchanging ball from one hand to the other. Stand with legs apart and shift weight from one side to the other with the movement of the ball.

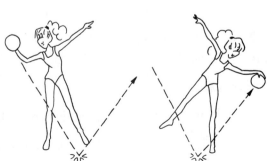

Variations:

√ Bounce ball holding a balance for a one second on each side

√ Kick leg forward and pass ball under leg with a bounce

√ Bounce ball while performing two cross steps to the right. Do the same to the left

√ Bounce ball, passing it behind body

√ Bounce ball, passing it between legs while lowering to a split. Catch ball with other hand

√ Bounce ball, passing it under legs during a scissors

√ Perform a split jump and pass ball under the legs with a bounce

√ Bounce ball in front of body in a kneeling position. Perform a side roll and catch with other hand

5) Bounce ball from back to front and vice versa, in oblique trajectory, in a kneeling position, catching ball in a deep lunge. Bounce ball backwards. Change hands.

Variations:

√ Bounce ball, do a forward roll and catch it with two hands

√ Hold a needle balance and bounce ball forward. Lower to floor and roll forward over shoulders. Catch ball in front with one hand, sitting on one foot with other leg extended forward

√ Stand with legs apart, weight on front leg. Bounce ball backwards and catch with one or two hands while holding a front balance

√ Bounce ball forward, catch with same hand in a vertical split balance, holding leg with free arm

c) Bounces with traveling steps.

1) Bounce ball with a chassé forward. Bounce at right side of body. Change hands and bounce at left side.

Variations:

√ Bounce ball twice during chassé. Step with third bounce and catch ball while doing a tuck jump

√ Bounce ball twice during the chassé. Push ball to the left during third bounce to pass ball under legs while doing a split leap

√ Do a side chassé and pass ball under legs, from rear to front, during a side split leap

d) <u>Bounces with other parts of the body.</u>

1) Bounces with knee. Bounce ball in front of body with one hand, then bounce on knee for the second. Bend knee upward in front of the body.

Variations:

√ Chassé with a bounce, then bounce on knee during a hop

√ Do previous element but with a tuck jump. Catch ball with a split leap

2) Bounce with foot. Do a small bounce in front of body and push second bounce with the sole of the foot, leg extended.

Variations:

√ Sitting, legs bent, bounce ball with foot in front of the body

√ Bounce ball with hand in front of body, turn 180° and do a second bounce with toe behind the body, leg bent

√ Chassé forward and bounce ball once. Do a split leap and bounce ball with foot during the leap

√ Same as previous element but bouncing ball on top of the foot, kicking it upward. Catch with the hand during a second split leap

3) Bounce with or on the chest. Bounce the ball in front of the body at arms length and above the level of the head. Arch the torso backwards to bounce the ball on the chest. Catch with one hand.

Variations:

√ Bounce with small steps forward. Hop on one leg, beating the legs together while in the air (cabriole) and bending the torso backwards to bounce the ball on the chest

√ Bounce the ball in front of the body. Hold a balance with a slight backward arch, and bounce the ball on the chest

√ Bounce the ball lightly in front of the body. Bend the torso forward to push the second bounce with the chest. Catch the ball on the back of both hands

4) Bounce with shoulder. Bounce ball in front of body above head height. Bounce ball on shoulder and catch with one hand.

Variations:

√ Bounce ball on floor, lunge forward to bounce on the shoulder

√ Bounce ball on floor, turn 180° and bounce on the shoulder

√ All the bounces of the ball which result from a throw will be studied in the section about throws

COMMON MISTAKES IN THE EXECUTION OF BOUNCES AND METHODS OF CORRECTION

a) Slapping the ball with noise

b) Involuntary variation in the direction of the bounce.

Methods of correction related to slapping the ball with noise

Noise is produced when the ball hits the hand as it is providing the downward impulse. When the ball contacts the hand, the hand must adopt the shape of the ball. The ball must not be gripped.

The arm is extended, not stiff, to bounce the ball as far from the body as possible. The arm follows the ball when pushing downward.

Exercise:

Place several hoops on the floor, draw circles with chalk, or use another method.

Bounce ball inside the circle:

   √ By hitting the ball with noise

   √ Without noise, hearing only the bounce of the ball on the floor

Repeat these exercises several times. Do high and low bounces, hitting the ball with noise and then without (repeat alternating the height of the bounce).

With these exercises the gymnasts learn how to handle the ball without noise. They will realize that it is easier to control the bounce by pushing the ball rather than by hitting it.

Perform the previous exercises with one hand, right and left, and then with two hands together.

Exercise:

With one hand after several bounces catch ball with back of hand and transfer to the other hand. Repeat the exercise.

With both hands at the same time, every two or three bounces push with the elbow.

Alternating hands, every three bounces bounce ball on one knee, pushing ball upward. (i.e.-Bounce with the right hand, left hand, right hand, and right knee; continue with a bounce with the left hand, right hand, left hand and left knee.)

Alternate one bounce with the hand and knee on one side (right), with and bounce with the hand and knee on the other side (left).

Method of correction related to involuntary variation in the direction of the bounce

The ball, after bouncing on the floor, does not rebound in the required direction. If the ball should rebound perpendicular to the floor, it rebounds oblique. If the ball should rebound oblique to one side, it rebounds in a different direction or perpendicular to the floor.

It is necessary for the palm of the hand to cover the ball and push on the top side of the ball to make the bounce perpendicular. If the ball is pushed on the right or left side or on the back or front side, the bounce will move in the opposite direction of the part which was pushed. Examples:

√ If the ball is pushed on its back side, it will move forward

√ If the ball is pushed on its right side, it will move to the left

√ If it is pushed on its front side, it will move backwards

Exercise:

Each gymnast has a ball and hoop placed on the floor in front of them.

Vertical bounces

Vertically in the center of the hoop, with one hand, with the other hand and with both simultaneously.

Bounces with lateral movement

Bounce ball once outside the hoop with right hand. For the second bounce push ball on the right side to bounce ball diagonally in center of hoop. Catch with left hand. Reverse the exercise starting with a vertical bounce outside the hoop with the left hand, then push diagonally on the left side, bouncing ball in the center of hoop and to the right. (Repeat several times).

Perform a continuous series of bounces with lateral movement from the right to the left and from the left to the right, without the vertical bounces outside the hoop.

Bounces with forward and backward movement

Same as the previous exercise with movement of the ball from the rear of the hoop to the front, or vice versa.

Combine the three exercises.

Bounce ball four times in center of hoop alternating right and left hands. When beginning the fifth bounce turn diagonally to the left and start four bounces with lateral movement, from right to left and from left to right. The fifth bounce is not as diagonal to keep ball vertical in center of hoop. Perform another four perpendicular bounces then push ball diagonally forward to start four bounces with forward and backward movement.

Game

Objective: To master the bounce.

Exercise: Each gymnast has her own ball and the necessary obstacles. The game consists of moving through the obstacles in an established form, completing the circuit as quickly as possible.

Use hoops, sport bags, clubs or ropes, folded mats, etc.:

Bounce ball inside hoop (with hands, elbow, foot, etc.).

Bounce ball moving around sport bags.

Bounce ball diagonally to the right and left between three or four clubs or ropes placed 50 cm apart.

Move around folded mats while bouncing ball on top of them with one hand or the other.

If the gymnast loses the ball or performs one of the stations incorrectly, she must go back to the beginning and start again.

The game can be adjusted according to the level of the gymnast as follows:

For beginners start with one point for each obstacle in the circuit. If the circuit has five obstacles, she starts with five points which will be subtracted, one at a time, every time the gymnast must return to the beginning. The game is over when the gymnast uses all her points.

For higher level gymnasts or for those who have mastered the game for beginners, the goal is to finish the circuit as quickly as possible.

ROTATIONS

In rotations the ball rotates on its vertical axis. The ball must not travel during rotations. This is considered a fault.

Rotations can be done on the floor or the body. The pushing for the rotation is done with the hand on top of the ball, spinning it to one direction or the other.

The ball can be picked up with one hand or both hands on the palm or the back of the hands. The fingertips contact the ball first, then the rest of the hand. Pick the ball up by placing one hand close to the contact point between the ball and the floor. Then, by using the fingers, the gymnast lifts the ball and rolls it onto the palm.

To increase the difficulty the gymnast may pick up the ball in the same manner using the back of her hand.

Rotations on the body can be done:

√ On palm of the hand   √ On the finger

√ On the chest   √ On the knees in front or back

Rotations on the floor

a) Kneeling, rotate ball in front of body with one hand. Do a large circumduction with the torso and pick up ball with two hands.

Variations:

√ Perform a knee spin during the rotation

√ Kneeling, rotate ball. Do a small jump to stand and pick up ball

√ Rotate ball, hold a balance on one knee, and pick up ball

√ Kneeling, do a pre-acrobatic movement (support on one arm, kick both legs, opening them in split) during the rotation

b) Sitting, rotate ball at right side of body.

Variations:

√ Rotate ball, perform a spin on the buttocks, passing the legs over the ball

√ Rotate ball, roll backwards and pick up ball

√ Rotate ball close to the body, do a fish flop

√ Rotate close to the body. Turn, leaving ball behind the body, and stand with a back arch to pick up ball with both hands

c) Standing, rotate ball and pass over it several times with small cross steps. Pick up ball with one hand.

Variations:

√ Rotate ball, perform a turn on one leg and pick up ball while kicking one leg backward to a vertical split position (needle)

√ Rotate ball in front of body, step forward and lower to the knees. Pick up ball with an arch backward

√ Rotate in a side lunge, perform a turn on the support leg with free leg extended to the side above head level. Pick up ball again in a side lunge

√ Rotate ball in front of the body, step forward and pick it up during a back scale

Rotations on the body

a) <u>Rotation on the knees.</u> Sit with legs together and bent. Rotate ball on knees, holding the balance on the buttock muscles.

Variations:

√ Pick up ball with two hands after performing alternating circles with the arms

√ At end of rotation, let ball roll down to the feet

√ Let ball roll toward hips, and by leaning torso backwards, roll ball up to and out arms

√ At end of rotation, separate knees and let ball bounce on the floor, catching under legs

√ Rotate ball on feet, sitting with legs flexed

b). <u>Rotations on the chest.</u> Place ball on chest, bending torso backwards and lunging on front leg. Pick up ball with two hands or one.

Variations:

√ Rotate ball holding balance on two legs, and perform circumductions with arms at the same time

√ Rotate ball holding a balance with free leg extended in front of body. Bend support leg and let ball roll out the arms

√ Rotate ball, legs together on the toes. Bend torso backwards and extend arms overhead, letting the ball roll out to the hands

c) <u>Rotations on palm of the hand.</u> Spin ball and stretch the hand to facilitate rotation on the hand. Rotate with arm stretched upward and lower to a kneeling position. Change hands.

Variations:

√ Rotate ball holding a balance with free leg behind body at a 45° angle

√ Rotate ball during a body wave

d) <u>Rotations on the finger, index or other.</u> Hold a lunge on the back leg. Change hands.

Variation:

√ Hold balance on the toes with both legs flexed during the rotation

e) <u>Rotations on one leg.</u> Lift one leg up to 90°, bent behind the body (back attitude). Rotate ball on side of knee while holding the balance. Change legs.

COMMON MISTAKES IN THE EXECUTION OF ROTATIONS AND METHODS OF CORRECTION

a) Travel of the ball during the rotation.

b) Excess or insufficient impulse.

Method of correction related to travel of the ball during the rotation

The ball moves in any direction away from the axis of rotation on which the ball must turn. This means that the rotational axis is not vertical during the impulse. It is caused by incorrect placement of the hand or by unequally distributing the impulse through the fingers.

The hand must initiate the rotation of the ball on the axis perpendicular to the floor. The fingers must be correctly placed, covering the entire top part of the ball, so that the impulse is equally applied by all the fingers.

Exercises:

Perform rotation of ball on the floor or body without letting go of the ball. Rotate ball with the hands in different ways to learn and to analyze how the movement is originated.

Examples:

√ Rotate with two, three, four or five fingers.

√ Place all fingers on the ball and do the rotation pushing only with:

- Fingers on the right side of the ball
- Fingers on the left side of the ball
- Fingers on the front of the ball
- Fingers on the back of the ball

Perform these exercises on the floor and body. The gymnast will observe that it is more difficult to rotate the ball with a few fingers, and that if the ball is pushed more on one side than the other, the ball will escape the hand to the sides.

Perform rotation with all the fingers, pushing equally on the top of the ball. After the rotation keep the hand in contact with the ball without moving it or disturbing its axis of rotation. If the ball escapes the hand, it is because the rotation is not correctly performed. The gymnast continues trying until the rotation is performed correctly, with each hand, on the floor and the body.

Rotate ball on the floor and perform any of a variety of elements:

√ Jump over the ball

√ Body wave

√ A turn, etc.

Rotate on the body:

√ Changing the position of the body (standing to sitting)

√ During traveling steps

√ Holding a balance, etc.

Methods of correction related to excess or insufficient impulse

If the ball receives too little push for the rotation, it will stop or roll along the body instead of rotating. It might also bounce or move away from the point of rotation.

The gymnast must provide proportionately adequate impulse for the rotation, allowing the gymnast to perform a specified body movement while the ball is spinning. The fingers must push the ball with equal force on its top surface to keep the ball from moving off its axis of rotation.

Exercises:

Do rotations with the right hand, exchange ball to the left hand and rotate again, stopping ball with the right hand. Repeat several times. Perform these exercises rotating the ball on the body, chest, palm of the hand, knees, and feet.

In pairs, rotate ball on the floor one at a time. The gymnast who is not rotating the ball counts the number of correctly completed exercises. Each gymnast must perform the following:

√ Small jumps over the ball during rotations

√ Rotate ball and place arms bent at sides of ball. Push with arms to extend torso upward lying in a prone position

√ Run around ball at different speeds

Game

Objective: To get the highest number of turns while rotating the ball correctly.

Exercise: This game is performed in groups of six gymnasts, each with a ball. The game consists of each group keeping the balls moving as long as possible.

The gymnasts form a circle, with the balls on the floor in front of each gymnast. When coach indicates the beginning of the game, all the gymnasts rotate the balls at the same time and start running around the balls using steps, short runs, jumps, or other traveling steps. When one of the balls stop rotating, the gymnast closest to it stops running while the others continue and so on, until all the gymnasts are stopped.

Exercise: Perform rotations on the body using one ball for every two gymnasts. One of them rotates the ball on the chest and her partner starts running as before (three pairs are playing).

Rotation Game

Each time a ball moves off its point of rotation (floor, body), the team loses one point. The group whose gymnast was the last one to stop receives one point. The goal is to build the largest number of points for the team.

ROLLS

Rolls are the group of elements most evident as a component of the basic technique of the ball. It is very difficult to control the travel of the ball when it rolls on the body. This difficulty decreases when the ball rolls on the floor. Rolls must be continuous and smooth and always in contact with the rolling surface.

Rolls can be done on the floor or on the body.

Rolls on the floor can be done with:

√ One hand   √ Both hands

√ One foot   √ Other part of the body (as long as it is held still)

Rolls on the floor can move:

√ To the right and left   √ To the front and back

√ In a curve   √ In a figure-eight

Rolls on the body can be done with:

√ One arm   √ Both arms

√ Chest   √ Back

√ Leg   √ Over the body lying prone

√ Over the body lying supine

Rolls on the body can move:

√ Up   √ Down

√ Front and back   √ Right and left

Rolls of the ball on the floor

a) Without travel or with little movement.

1) In a kneeling position seated on the toes, roll ball in front of body from right to left and vice versa with the same hand. Use the other hand.

Variations:

√ Exchange ball from one hand to the other

√ Coordinate with arm waves

√ Roll ball, lifting the knees so ball passes under the knees

√ Roll ball behind the body

√ Roll ball, do a side roll and catch ball

2) In a kneeling position seated on toes, roll ball in the sagittal plane from back to front with one hand. Change the direction. Coordinate with arm waves. Change hands.

Variations:

√ Alternate rolls with right and left

√ Coordinate with arm circumductions in the sagital plane

√ Roll front and back with knees apart and lifting hips to pass ball under body. Catch ball behind body with a twist of the torso

√ Roll back to front, lowering body to a front support. Catch ball with hands and roll backwards, stopping ball with feet

√ Roll back to front, perform a roll forward and catch ball with one hand

3) Sitting with the legs together and extended, lift legs to a "V" position and roll ball under the legs.

Variations:

√ Support feet on the floor and roll ball in a circle around the body

√ Legs together and extended on the floor, hold ball with one foot on top. Roll ball backwards and roll the body back, lifting hips and legs to the vertical (shoulder stand). Catch ball with two hands behind back

√ With legs apart and extended, lift hips with support on one hand. Roll ball backwards passing it between legs, under body and past the head. Return to a seated position and lower to lie supine to catch ball.

√ Sitting, roll behind body, left to right. Perform an acro jump to the right and catch ball in a kneeling position

4) Kneeling on one knee with other leg extended in front of body, roll to left passing ball under the leg. Lower to a split, then to a prone position to catch ball with two hands.

Variations:

√ Pass through split to a seated position, catching ball with the feet

√ Pass through split to a front support, stopping ball with one hand

5) Lying prone, roll ball from right to left and vice versa, exchanging ball from one hand to the other with each roll under the chest. Perform arm waves.

Variations:

√ Roll ball, kick back leg and catch leg with one hand. Catch ball with the other hand

√ Roll ball from hands to feet passing it under the body by lifting the hips. Catch ball with the feet

6) Lying supine, roll from right to left passing ball under the shoulders. Supporting with the hands on the floor, lift chest with the head inclined backwards.

Variations:

√ Roll ball parallel to the body from feet toward the head. Roll backwards to a kneeling position and catch ball with hands

√ Same as the previous exercise, but performing a fish-flop

√ Roll from hands overhead toward the back of the body. Bend the legs to a sitting position then stand with a deep arch to catch ball with both hands

√ Same as the previous exercise, but standing up with a backscale

7) Standing, with side lunges roll ball in front of body from right to left and vice versa, changing hands.

Variations:

√ Roll, perform a side body wave and catch ball with the other hand

√ Roll, do a small cat step and catch with the other hand

√ Roll in a figure-eight pattern between the legs, alternating hands

8) Forward lunge, roll ball backwards and shift weight to a backward lunge. Roll forward and return to the forward lunge. Change hands.

Variations:

√ Roll backward and forward kicking one leg backward to the vertical to hold a needle position

√ Roll forward and stop the ball with one foot. Roll backward with the foot and stop it with the same foot

b) <u>Rolls with traveling movements.</u>

1) Roll ball forward with forward crossed steps, stepping over the ball. Pick up ball with two hands in front of the body.

Variations:

√ Circle step over the ball

√ Jump over ball from one side to the other with small running steps

√ Roll the ball, perform a waltz step forward

√ Jump over ball with cabriole jumps to one side and the other

2) Large roll forward with travel, perform a chassé then tuck jump over the ball, turn 180° to pick up ball with one or two hands.

Variations:

√ Perform a tuck jump with half turn over ball

√ Perform a forward leap over ball, catch in kneeling position

3) Large roll to left with travel, jump over ball with a side leap, and pick up ball with backs of the hands.

Variations:

√ Perform a fouetté hop over ball and pick up ball with backs of the hands

√ Perform a tour jeté and pick up ball with back of one hand

√ Perform a jump over one leg and pick up ball with back of one or two hands

4) Large roll forward with travel, jump over ball and pick up with an inward rotation of the arm. Lift arm to a normal position and roll ball up on the outside of the arm.

Variations:

√ Roll ball, jump over it with double stag and prepare for forward roll on the floor. Pick up ball on the palm of the hand with arm rotated inward and perform forward roll

√ Roll ball and jump over it with a tour jeté. Pick up ball behind body with arm rotated inward, then throw ball forward to the other hand

5) Roll ball backwards and hold a balance in arabesque. Turn 180°, perform a chassé and a turning leap to pick up ball with two hands.

Variations:

√ Roll ball. Kick leg backward to hold a balance in vertical split, holding leg with one hand. Turn 180° in this position, then chassé and jump over ball with a turning leap and kneel to pick up ball

√ Roll ball, perform one turning leap then a second turning leap finishing on the floor to catch the ball

c) Rolling the body over the ball.

1) Roll forward on ball from a kneeling position. Bend body forward and roll body over ball from chest to legs.

Variation:

√ Lower body to the ground from a needle scale position, keeping arms on floor and rolling from chest to feet

2) Roll ball forward, chassé and slide forward onto the ball rolling along body to the feet. Use both arms for support.

Variation:

√ After the roll, lower body to the floor and turn 180° right. Lift legs and roll ball from feet to chest

Rolls of the ball on the body

a) Roll on the arms.

1) Roll between hands. With arms bent in front of body, place ball on back of one hand and hold with palm of the other hand on the opposite side of the ball. Rotate ball forward and backward between the hands.

Variations:

√ Roll ball with legs in demi-plié and body inclined forward. Lift body progressively to full extension

√ Coordinate with a forward body wave

√ Hold balance on both legs, but finish extension on one leg

√ Coordinate with a large side bend

√ Roll while doing a waltz step

2) Roll ball on palms of hands. Place arms vertically overhead with ball on palms. Transfer ball from one hand to the other, rolling over the fingers.

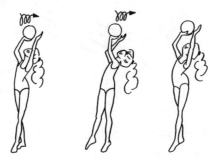

Variations:

√ Cordinate with little running steps forward

√ Hold a balance position

3) Roll on two arms. Hold ball with both hands, arms stretched in front of the body. Raise arms to 135° (approximately) to start ball rolling toward the chest. Lower arms to roll ball back to hands. Raise them again as ball reaches the hands. Ball must not touch wrists when held.

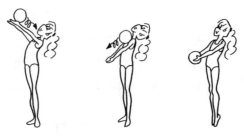

Variations:

√ Coordinate with rhythmic steps

√ Roll ball to chest and suspend it there by bending the torso backwards. Do a backward circumduction with the arms before rolling ball over arms out to hands

√ Lunge step forward during first part of roll. Lower body over toes to the knees during second part of roll

4) Roll on one arm. Hold ball on one hand with arm extended horizontally in front of body. Roll ball to shoulder and stop it with the other hand. Roll ball out along the same arm toward the hand.

Variations:

√ Roll ball to shoulder. Perform a backward arm circumduction and return to starting position to roll ball to the hand

√ Hold an arabesque during the second roll

√ Hold a balance, changing position of the free leg in the second roll

5) Roll on one arm and hand. Hold ball on one hand, arm vertical with torso arched backwards. Roll ball to shoulder and stop it with the other hand. Lower rolling arm and place it in front of the body to roll ball out to the hand.

Variations:

√ Perform small steps backwards during roll and kick one leg backward as ball reaches hand

√ Lower to knees during first roll. Bend torso forward to finish roll

√ Do a waltz step forward with a turn. Roll ball to shoulder during first half turn and roll to the hand during second half turn

b) Roll on arms and torso (chest, back).

1) Roll on arms and chest. With arms extended and slightly forward roll ball from one hand to the other across chest. Hold arms in place during the roll. To learn

this roll, first roll ball to the shoulder and stop it with one hand. Exchange to the other shoulder, then roll to other hand.

Variations:

√ Roll ball from left to right and vice versa, performing a wave with the arm after the ball passes over it

√ Perform small steps in relevé forward and backward

√ Hold a balance on one leg with the other one bent to the back with knees together

√ Perform a turn on one leg in the same position as the previously mentioned balance when starting the roll

√ For a higher difficulty, roll ball during a split leap

2) Roll on arms and back. Roll ball with arms extended to the sides from one hand to the other, passing it behind the head. (Same sequence as roll across chest).

Variations:

√ Coordinate roll with a forward lunge

√ Kneel and roll ball with torso bent slightly forward

√ Roll ball from right hand to left during a turn left on the right leg

3) Roll from one arm to the other over the chest. Hold one arm in front of the body with other arm extended overhead and to the rear. Roll ball over chest from the hand in back to the one in front. Bend head backward to make roll easier and keep palms of hands facing up.

Variations:

√ Roll while stepping to a forward lunge

√ Roll backward, from the hand in front to the one in back, with a back arch

√ Roll backward to finish in a back scale

4) Roll on arms with hands together forming a circle in front of the body. Push ball with the elbows as it passes over them.

Variations:

√ Coordinate with small rhythmic steps forward

√ Roll ball over nape of the neck by lowering head between the arms

5) Roll on back bending the torso forward. Place ball on nape of neck with both hands. Roll ball down back to the tailbone and catch with two hands.

Variations:

√ Roll ball down back and bend legs to sit over the ball. With ball placed under legs, throw ball upward with the feet.

√ Roll ball over arms extended to the front. Lower head between the arms to roll ball over the neck and shoulders and continue roll down the back

6) Roll on back from tailbone to shoulders and arms. Bend body forward to horizontal, place ball on the tailbone and push it to roll up back and shoulders.

Variations:

√ Make roll longer by rolling ball over the arms placed horizontally in front of the body after roll up the back

√ Kneeling, roll ball from tailbone to hands then roll on the ball over the chest, torso and hips

7) Roll ball upward over the chest to shoulders then roll down the back to tailbone.

Variations:

√ Perform roll with a body wave

√ Roll over right arm to shoulder and catch ball behind with left arm

√ Hold a balance on one leg (extended) with free leg at 45° when ball rolls up chest. Close legs together in demi-plié when ball rolls down back

8) Roll ball up one side of body to hand on the opposite side. Hold ball with right hand against right side of the body. In a left side lunge roll ball to chest and across to the left arm and out to left hand.

Variations:

√ Roll ball while holding a balance

√ Finish roll with a side bend

√ Perform roll in a kneeling position and extend right leg to the side during roll

9) Roll up one side of body to hand on the same side. Hold ball against right side of body with right hand. Roll ball up to the right hand while bending the torso to the left.

Variation:

√ Roll with a side lunge

10) Roll over chest, arms and hands. Place ball on chest and roll out to hands by arching the body backward with arms extended overhead.

Variations:

√ Roll with little running steps

√ Roll while lowering to knees

√ Roll with back scale

c) <u>Rolls on the legs.</u>

    1) Sit with legs extended and together. Roll ball from feet to hips and back to feet. Start roll by lifting legs, and lift hips to roll ball back toward the feet.

Variations:

    √ Roll from hips to feet, lift feet and legs and throw ball to the hands

    √ Make roll longer by bending the torso upward as the ball reaches the chest to roll ball out arms to hands

    √ Lying in a supine position roll ball from hands to feet, passing over the arms, chest, hips and legs. Lift arms to start the roll

    2) Lying on the stomach, roll ball from hips to feet. Lift legs to roll ball back to the hips.

Variations:

    √ Roll ball from nape of the neck impulsed by the hands. Bend knees when ball reaches them. Turn body to a sitting position and catch ball under legs with one hand

    √ Roll ball from buttocks to the feet. Lift legs to throw ball toward hands when ball reaches the feet

COMMON MISTAKES IN THE EXECUTION OF ROLLS AND METHODS OF CORRECTION

    a) Bounces during rolls.

    b) Incomplete rolls.

Methods of correction related to bounces during rolls

    The ball does not roll over the entire rolling surface and misses some parts. The movement of the ball must be continuous and smooth, moving without bouncing along the whole rolling surface. The rolling movement must be accompanied by the body to avoid incomplete rolls on the body.

Exercise with rolls on the floor:

Split group in pairs with one ball per pair. Pass ball to the partner by rolling it on the ground in different directions. The partner always starts standing beside the gymnast who is rolling the ball.

Pass ball to the partner by rolling it slowly in any direction. Follow the movement of the ball with the arm and hand until the ball is rolling freely on the floor. Progressively increase the speed of the roll. One of the gymnasts rolls the ball and the other one moves to catch the ball before it stops.

With a slow roll, the partner walks slowly close to the ball. When the speed of the roll increases the rhythm of the walk also increases. When the ball rolls fast the partner must start running to catch the ball before it reaches the wall of the gym.

Perform rolls with both right and left hands from different positions, standing, sitting, kneeling, lying down, etc. The partner starts from the same position as the gymnast who performs the roll.

Use all directions, forward, backward and sideward. Change tasks so the other gymnast performs the roll.

Other exercises:

√ Sitting, lift legs extended and roll ball from right to left, passing ball under them

√ Perform the same exercise lying in a prone position. Lift torso and roll ball under chest

√ Sitting on heels, shift weight onto the feet to lift knees and roll ball under them

Exercises with rolls on the body

Roll ball between hands. Start slowly and pay attention to the feel of the ball in contact with the hands.

Sit with legs extended and together. One gymnast rolls ball down her legs toward legs of her partner, keeping toes pointed and close to the floor. Partner lets the ball roll up her legs to the hips, assisting roll with hands at the sides of the ball. She then lifts her hips and rolls ball down her legs to return it to the first gymnast.

Lying in a prone position, one gymnast places the ball on her feet. Smoothly lift the legs so the ball rolls to the buttocks where it is stopped with the hands. The gymnast then pushes the ball to roll it down her legs and to her partner's feet. Reverse tasks.

Stand with arms extended in front of body. Hold ball on one hand and smoothly lift arm without bending wrist to roll ball along arm to the shoulder. Catch it with the other hand. Help ball to roll over shoulder then release to roll down back. Catch with both hands. Perform both movements without stopping ball on the shoulder, over two arms together. When ball reaches the shoulders lower arms to roll ball down back and catch with hands. Also perform this exercise with right and left arm.

Methods of correction related to incomplete rolls

The ball does not travel along the entire rolling surface. Rolls are made short when the gymnast anticipates the catch, trying to avoid dropping the ball or holding it static. The gymnast must provide the correct impulse to the ball at the beginning of the roll, so the ball can complete its travel without help of the fingers. The rolling surface must be smooth to avoid any interruptions during the travel of the ball.

Exercise with rolls on the floor:

Draw parallel lines on the floor (ropes, chalk lines, etc). Perform short rolls from one partner to the other between the two lines spaced 3 feet away. Roll ball from one line to the other and catch before it touches the line. Increase the distance between the lines to 6, 9, 12 feet, etc.

Perform different exercises during the roll such as:

√ Touch floor with both hands   √ Sit and stand quickly

√ Straight jump or split jump   √ Lie on back or stomach

√ Cartwheel

Use both hands.

Other exercises:

Sit with legs extended and together, one gymnast next to her partner. Place one hand on the floor and roll ball with the other hand. The partner stops the ball, pushes it back in the opposite direction. Lift hips allowing ball to pass under.

Kneel with knees apart. One gymnast is placed in front of the other facing the same direction. The first gymnast rolls ball backward between legs of both gymnasts. The second gymnast catches ball by arching the torso backward. She then rolls the ball forward (starting with the ball behind her) between the legs. The first gymnast catches it by bending the torso forward.

Lying in a prone position with one gymnast ahead of the other, roll ball from hands to feet, lifting each part of the body successively to roll ball underneath. The second gymnast catches ball with her hands and performs the same movement. Next, roll ball from hands of the first gymnast to the feet of her partner without stopping ball.

Exercises with rolls over the body:

These rolls are performed with three gymnasts in a row. Pass ball from first gymnast to the second and then to the third. The first gymnast then moves around to become the fourth person and so on. In some exercises the first and second gymnasts will be facing each other. The second girl then must turn 180° to face the third girl and so on. Repeat each roll 15 or 20 times.

Lying in a prone position, roll ball from hips to the feet. The next gymnast catches ball with hands to place it on her hips and repeat the exercise.

Lying in a supine position, roll ball from stomach to hands with the back arched. Finish with arms inclined to facilitate the roll out to the hands. The second gymnast catches ball in a sitting position and then lays down to begin the roll. The feet of the first gymnast should be one foot away from the head of the second gymnast.

Standing, place ball on the nape of the neck and roll down back with torso bent forward. The second gymnast catches ball when it reaches the tailbone. This gymnast performs the roll, the third one catches it and so on. The first gymnast moves to the end of the line by either walking or running.

Standing with torso bent forward parallel to floor, place ball on tailbone and roll ball toward the head. The second gymnast is situated in front of the first to catch ball. She turns 180° to face the third gymnast and rolls ball up the back. Once this element has been mastered, make the roll longer, rolling ball from tailbone over the back, head and arms.

Kneeling and seated on heels, place ball on the chest and roll it up to one shoulder using both hands. The second gymnast catches ball from the shoulder of her partner and performs the roll to pass ball to the third gymnast and so on.

Roll ball from chest, over one shoulder and down back by bending torso forward to 90°. The second gymnast catches ball and performs the roll to the third gymnast.

Standing, roll ball from chest, over the head and out to the hands with arms extended overhead and torso arched backward. The second gymnast catches ball and performs the roll.

Standing, roll ball from one shoulder over the arms to the hands. Place ball on the shoulder of the next gymnast to roll it over arms to the hands and so on. This roll starts from the back of the line and moves forward.

Standing, roll ball from hands to the shoulders and back to the hands. The second gymnast, standing in front of the first, catches ball and turns 180°. She performs the roll facing the third gymnast.

Game

Objective: To improve amplitude of rolls and group dynamics.

Exercise: Divide into groups of four gymnasts with one ball per group. The game constists of rolling the ball through the four girls in both directions using four body positions, lying on the floor, seated, kneeling and standing.

The four girls are placed in a row, at the same distance from each other. The first gymnast, lying in a supine position, pushes the ball with both hands from the chest

An Example of a Rolling Game

An Example of a Rolling Game

and up the arms to the hands. The back must arch, lifting the chest, to roll ball out the arms extended backward and overhead.

The second gymnast, seated behind the first gymnast, catches the ball and performs the same rolling movement by extending the torso backward to pass ball to the third gymnast.

The third gymnast, in a kneeling position, performs the same exercise to pass to the fourth and last gymnast.

The fourth gymnast performs the exercise in a standing position. When the ball reaches her hands, she signals the rest of the group to turn 90° right to form a row.

At this point the ball begins its return to the first gymnast in the following manner. The fourth gymnast holds the ball in her right hand with the arms extended to the sides. The rest of the girls also hold their arms in this position. The fourth gymnast performs a roll along her right arm, across her chest and out the left arm.

The third gymnast catches the ball and performs the roll in her kneeling position. The exercise continues as before, passing the ball to the second then the first gymnast.

When the first gymnast finishes this roll, she holds the ball in her left hand until the fourth gymnast (who was standing) moves to lie in a supine position and becomes the first gymnast. All the gymnasts then move, changing their positions to form a row, to begin the exercise again.

Repeat with a turn to the left to roll the ball back down the row from left to right across the chest.

The game is over when the gymnasts have performed the rolls in each position in line. The gymnasts must continue to attempt the roll until it is performed correctly. The goal is for the team to finish in the least amount of time.

For the highest level of difficulty, each gymnast must perform a different roll in each position.

Note: Rolls on the floor are not included in this game since they are less difficult than rolls on the body and require less training to perfect. However, using the same system, the coach can adapt many different combinations of rolls on the floor and on the body with other groups of elements such as bounces, throws, etc.

THROWS AND CATCHES

Throws and catches with the ball have numerous variations. In all cases the ball must be thrown by stretching both the arm and the body. The fingertips are the last parts of the body to be in contact with the ball when throwing, and the first parts to contact the ball when catching.

Forms of throwing:

√ With one hand — palm or back of hand, with or without travel

√ With two hands — palms or backs of hands, crossed or uncrossed

√ With the feet

√ To the front, back or side

√ Starting from a push, swing, circumduction, roll

√ With different displacement — vertical high or low, horizontal short or long

Forms of catching:

√ With one hand — palm or back of hand

√ With two hands — palms or backs of hands, crossed or uncrossed

√ With the feet

√ Throw and catch-after a bounce, without bouncing

Throws with the hands

a) <u>Throws from two hands.</u>

1) Coordinate a throw in front of the body with flexion and extension of the legs. Catch ball with both hands in a mixed position, palm of one hand and back of the other.

Variations:

√ Throw, circle arms backward in the sagittal plane and catch

√ Throw and catch, coordinated with forward rhythmic steps

√ Throw and catch while performing a side waltz step

√ Throw and catch while holding a balance

2) Throw with hands crossed. Hold ball in both hands with arms crossed. Throw ball upward, opening arms and crossing them again quickly to catch. Coordinate with flexion and extension of the legs.

Variations:

√ Perform short running steps with two successive throws

√ Throw, hold a balance position and catch

√ Throw, step under ball to catch behind the body with both hands

3) Hold ball with both hands behind the body. Throw ball upward with a flexion and extension of the legs. Catch ball again behind the body with one or both hands.

Variations:

√ Throw, turn 180° and catch with backs of hands in front of body

√ Throw, lower to the knees and catch with two hands with torso arched backward

√ Throw with small cat step, turn 180° letting ball bounce and catch in arabesque balance

4) Throw ball from behind body over the head to the front. Hold ball with both hands, arms extended behind the body. Throw ball forward to catch with backs of both hands, coordinated with a flexion and extension of the legs.

Variations:

√ Throw forward, catch in arabesque with arms extended forward

√ Throw forward, catch during a split leap with one hand

√ Throw forward with a back leg kick, forward roll and catch ball seated with two hands

5) Stand holding ball with both feet. Jump and bend knees behind the body to throw ball upward. Catch with one or two hands.

b) <u>Throws from one hand.</u>

1) Throw from one hand to the other over the head. From a side lunge throw ball from one hand to the other while shifting weight from one leg to the other.

Variations:

√ Throw from one side to the other with running steps forward. Incline torso to the side when catching

√ Throw, turn 180° and catch with the same hand

√ Throw, perform a small cat step and catch

√ Throw, catch while holding a balance in arabeque

2) Throw ball from one hand to the other from behind body to the right and left.

Variations:

√ Throw from one hand to the opposite shoulder (may be followed by roll down the arm)

√ Throw from one hand under the free arm, catch with either hand

√ Combine a throw from behind to catch in front with other hand and a throw in front changing hands. Coordinate with a waltz step

√ Throw under the leg with leg lifted in front of the body in a bent position. Catch with the other hand

3) Throw ball with an internal rotation of the arm, catch with the same hand.

Variations:

√ Throw with one hand to the other over the head

√ Throw in kneeling position and perform a side roll. Catch when lying on the back and continue the roll

√ Throw during a split leap with right or left hand and catch with the same hand

4) Throw high over the head with one hand and catch with one or two hands. Coordinate with a flexion and extension of the legs.

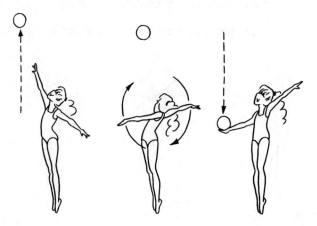

Variations:

√ Throw, perform successive arm circumductions backward in the sagittal plane, catch with one hand

√ Throw, perform a 360° turn, catch with two hands

√ Throw, perform a front balance, catch with one hand

√ Same as previous, catch in a back scale

√ Throw ball with kick of leg backward to catch leg with one hand in a vertical split. Catch ball with a back arch, legs together, continuing descent of the ball

√ Throw, perform a backscale and lower to the ground with a half turn. Let ball bounce and catch with one or two hands in a position on the floor

5) Throw ball in front of body and catch with palm or back of the same or opposite hand. Perform successive backward arm circumductions.

Variations:

√ Throw, perform a forward lunge with the arm circumductions and return to original position to catch

√ Throw, arch backward with arm waves and stand to catch

√ Kneel on one leg, other leg bent with the toes on the floor. Throw ball upward, perform a knee spin, catch with the other hand

√ Seated, throw ball upward. Perform a seat spin and catch ball with one hand

c) Throws with travel.

1) Throw ball high with one hand, moving forward. Catch with one or two hands. Coordinate with flexion and extension of the legs. Perform small runs forward on the toes with arm movements.

Variations:

√ Throw forward, forward roll, catch with two hands after a bounce

√ Throw forward, perform a split leap, catch with two hands during a tuck jump

√ Throw forward during a split leap, catch during another leap

√ Throw during a jump, land and perform a roll on the floor, catch with a back arch

√ Throw during a ring leap, run forward and lower to the knees to catch on the backs of the hands

√ Throw, perform a forward roll while the ball bounces in front of the body. Perform a side roll and catch with one hand

2) Throw ball high with one hand, moving backward. Perform a backward waltz step. Let the ball bounce then catch in a forward lunge.

Variations:

√ Throw, perform a backward roll over the shoulder and let ball bounce in front of body. Catch with a balance on two feet

√ Throw, perform a side leap, let ball bounce behind the body and catch to continue the turn after the side leap

√ Throw, perform a turning leap. Let ball bounce and perform a second turning leap. Catch with one hand

Throws with the feet

Variations:

√ Sit with legs extended and together. Roll ball toward feet and throw by lifting both legs

√ Sit with legs apart and bent with ball between the feet. Throw upward to catch overhead

√ Lying in a prone position with ball between the feet, flex legs to throw ball forward and catch with one hand

√ Sit with legs bent and ball between feet. Throw ball upward and catch with an arch rise

COMMON MISTAKES IN THE EXECUTION OF THROWS AND METHODS OF CORRECTION

a) Excessive bending of the arm when throwing or catching the ball.

b) Interruption of the natural trajectory of the ball.

Methods of correction related to excessive bending of the arm when throwing or catching ball

The result is that the ball loses contact with hand before throw and the arm is late to meet ball for catch. The body and arm must accompany ball to a fully extended position before the ball loses contact with hand. The body and arm must also be fully extended to catch the ball.

Exercise:

Start the movement of the ball with a swing. Try to throw the ball higher than an object which is placed higher for each repetition (hoop, rope, bars, etc.) After the throw, hold the position and wait to catch ball. A height of three feet is sufficient for this exercise.

Methods of correction related to interruption of the natural trajectory of the ball

The trajectory is interrupted when the movement of the ball is stopped immediately by the hand when catching. The result is a noisy catch or gripping the ball to keep it from bouncing off the hand. The ball should contact hand with the body and arm totally extended. Ball moves with the arm during the swing and continues movement into the next exercise.

Exercises:

Throw ball from one gymnast to the next using arm swings and without stopping the movement. Perform with the following variations:

√ Throw forward   √ Throw sideward

√ Throw backward   √ Throw from back to front

√ Throw with two hands √ Throw with one hand

Throw from different starting positions:

√ Lying on back

√ Sitting

√ Kneeling

√ Lunge

√ With flexion of the torso

Game

Objective: To develop the ability to throw a ball to a specific height in a specific direction.

Exercise: Divide into groups of six or eight gymnasts, one hoop and one ball per group. The game consists of throwing the ball through the hoop as many times as possible in a limited time (five to ten minutes) without stopping movement of the ball.

The gymnasts stand in a circle. One gymnast stands in the center of the circle with arms extended holding the hoop overhead with two hands. The hoop is raised throughout the game by placing the center gymnast on stacked mats, a table, etc. The gymnast with the hoop always faces the girl with the ball and holds the hoop open to this girl and perpendicular to the floor.

Throw the ball through the hoop with the following:

√ Forward with two hands

√ Sideward with one hand

√ Forward with the backs of both hands

√ Forward with arms crossed

√ Backward with two hands

√ Backward with one hand

Catch the ball as follows:

√ One or two hands (palm or back) after a bounce

√ Two hands

√ One hand (right and left)

√ Two hands crossed

Ball Toss Game

Each member of the group takes turns holding the hoop. The object is to throw the ball through the hoop as many times as possible in a certain amount of time. The throw does not count if the ball is dropped or caught incorrectly.

BALANCING THE BALL ON THE HAND

This group of elements is based on maintaining the ball in balance, either on the palm or back of the hand. When handling the ball it must not lose contact with the hand or hands for even a split second, and it must not come in contact with the wrist or any other part of the body.

The ball may be handled with the palm or back of the hand and both are combined with elements of rhythmic floor.

a) <u>Balance ball in the palm of the hand.</u>

1) Place ball in the palm of one hand with arms extended to the sides. Perform several internal and external rotations of the arm with the ball.

Variations:

√ Coordinate with rhythmic steps

√ Hold a balance

√ Coordinate a cabriole right with internal rotation, cabriole left with external rotation

√ Coordinate with a waltz step

2) Hold ball in one hand, arms extended in front of the body. Perform a small inward circle from the elbow moving the ball under the shoulder and to the front. Continue with a large horizontal circumduction. Change hands.

Variations:

√ Accompany the movement with a body wave

√ Kneeling, perform the movement with a back arch with support from the free hand

√ Standing, bend torso forward with small circle, backscale with large circumduction

√ Coordinate with a turn on two feet

√ Complete small circle, combine large circumduction with a turn on one foot

3) Hold ball in right hand with arm extended in front of body. Perform a small inward circle from the elbow moving ball under shoulder and to the front.

Exchange ball to left hand and continue with a large horizontal circumduction to the left. The second arm may receive ball with an inward rotation or in a normal position.

Variations:

√ Perform small steps with small circle, forward lunge with circumduction

√ In a kneeling position, perform small circle. Exchange ball and support with free hand to perform a preacrobatic movement with the circumduction

b) <u>Balance ball on back of hand.</u>

1) Balance ball on backs of two hands and move the arms up and down in front of the body. Coordinate with flexion and extension of the legs.

Variations:

√ Coordinate with small runs in a waltz rhythm

√ Coordinate with a turn on two legs

√ Lower to a kneeling position over the toes

2) Balance ball on the back of one hand. Extend the arm to front or side of body.

Variations:

√ Travel in a circle with ball as the center

√ Hold a balance

COMMON MISTAKES IN THE EXECUTION AND METHODS OF CORRECTION

a) Imprecision when balancing ball on hand.

b) Contact of ball with a part the body.

Methods of correction related to imprecision when balancing ball

The ball is moving around on the hand which forces the arm and hand to move to avoid dropping the ball. The hand must adapt to the shape of the ball.

Exercises:

Hold ball on back of one hand and with arm extended, move ball slowly and smoothly to the right and left (change hands).

Flex and extend the legs smoothly, moving the arm up and down legs (change hands).

Combine these exercises while exchanging the ball from hand to hand. With ball on back of right hand, move right arm to the right side and back to the front. Exchange ball to left hand coordinated with bending of the legs. Extend legs and repeat exercise to the left.

Maintain ball in balance while stepping over different objects (gym bags, stacked mats, other gymnasts). Hold ball with one hand then the other, changing after each object.

Perform these exercises holding ball with palm of one hand alternating the forearm position (internal or external rotation of the forearm).

Accompany each change of grip with flexion and extension of the legs. Change ball from palm (normal arm position) to back of hand with internal rotation of forearm, to a balance position on the palm with a second internal rotation. Return to a normal position with external rotation. Repeat the exercise several times. Change hands.

Methods of correction related to contact of the ball with the body

During movements the ball shifts on the hand and is held against a part of the body (usually the wrist and forearm) to avoid dropping. The movement of the arm must be very slow with maximum amplitude. The hand must always remain parallel to the floor. Avoid bending the wrist which causes the ball to shift.

Exercise:

Kneeling with knees apart (for better stability), bend torso forward with free hand on the floor. Arm holding ball is extended. Move extended arm to the right and left sides with ball on the palm of the hand. The arm moves parallel to the floor.

Increase the movement each time to complete half a circle. Increase to perform a complete circle followed by an internal or external rotation of the arm to continue the circle in the same direction.

Perform these circles:

√ With right and left arms

√ From right to left and vice versa

√ With horizontal circles under the arm (these movements are done with continuous and slow rotation of the forearm, ball balanced on the palm of one hand)

It is important to keep the elbow as far from the body as possible to make the circles close to the body easier. If necessary use a partner to assist the gymnast by gently pulling the elbow forward to achieve a greater amplitude.

Other exercises:

Move ball forward and backward several times under the arm, balanced on the palm.

Continue the movement back and forth around a full circle.

After the circle, change ball to palm of hand with an external rotation of the forearm and continue movement in the same direction.

After the circle, exchange ball to palm of the other hand, receiving the ball with the forearm in a normal position, and continue the movement.

Game

Objective: To maintain the ball in balance on the hand without gripping or contacting any part of the body.

Exercise: Use different items as obstacles (hoops, chairs, gym bags, seated gymnasts, etc.) placed around the floor area. Play music with no change of rhythm for accompaniment. The gymnasts must move the ball around the obstacles while keeping the ball balanced on the hand.

The gymnasts move around the floor with running steps, turns, etc. maintaining the ball in balance. They must stop in front of each obstacle and perform a movement balancing the ball on the hand which carries the ball completely around the obstacle.

The game consists of performing a different type of movement at each obstacle and moving through the entire floor in the least amount of time. The movements must be performed correctly with precision and without the ball touching a part of the body. Perform the movements with maximum amplitude. (Examples: circle under the arm, over the head, in a support position on the floor, on the back of the hand, etc.) The movements must be performed with both hands (right, left) at each obstacle.

Movements are not accepted if:

√ The movement is short and does not encompass the obstacle

√ The ball is held against a part of the body

√ The ball is dropped

MUSICAL ACCOMPANIMENT

The ball is the most expressive apparatus and requires full, fluid music with a 3/4 rhythm, for example. This helps the gymnast to prolong the body movements with maximum amplitude, finishing with the ball movement.

The music must be carefully selected and interpreted to create perfect synchronization.

Utilize the fast arpeggios in the music to perform throws, and the parts with strongly marked rhythms to execute bounces.

Do not discard other types of music, however, because some gymnasts have difficulty adapting to these rhythms. In this case utilize compositions with faster tempos.